G000141639

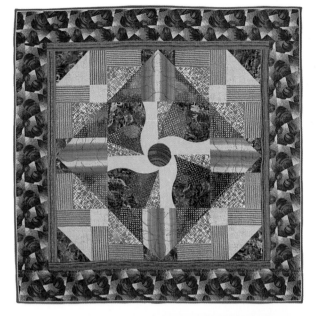

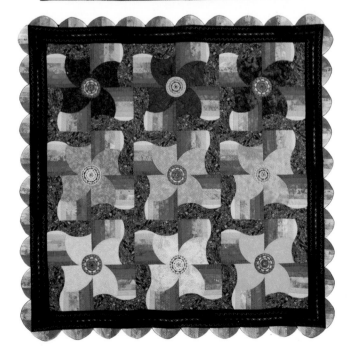

Spinning Pinwheel Quilts

Sara Moe

©2007 Sara Moe

Published by

kp krause publications

An Imprint of F+W Publications

700 East State Street • Iola, WI 54990-0001
715-445-2214 • 888-457-2873
www.krausebooks.com

Our toll-free number to place an order or obtain
a free catalog is (800) 258-0929.

All rights reserved. No portion of this publication may be reproduced or transmitted in any form or by any means, electronic or mechanical, including photocopy, recording, or any information storage and retrieval system, without permission in writing from the publisher, except by a reviewer who may quote brief passages in a critical article or review to be printed in a magazine or newspaper, or electronically transmitted on radio, television, or the Internet.

The following registered trademark terms and companies appear in this publication: 3-6-9 Design System and all related products and techniques, Adobe Reader, Bernina, Blank Textiles, Dritz, Herbal Essences, Husqvarna Viking, Microtex, Mylar, Pfaff, Reflexions, Steam-a-Seam, Sulky Holoshimmer, Sulky Soft 'n Sheer, Superior Glitter, VSM, Wonder Tape, Wonder Under, W.H. Collins, X-ACTO.

Library of Congress Control Number: 2007923004

ISBN-13: 978-0-89689-559-1
ISBN-10: 0-89689-559-9

Edited by Andy Belmas
Designed by Katrina Newby

Printed in China

Acknowledgments

For years while working in the corporate world as an account executive for a major computer company, I dreamed of a career that would let me pursue my passion for sewing, fabric and art. But I never expected I would be living out this dream at this point in my life. Sewing has been a hobby of mine since I was in the seventh grade, and I was always a "wanna be" artist. Some days I wake up and feel like I need to pinch myself, to make sure that I am not dreaming the life I have been living for the past five years. My career in the sewing and quilting industry has been an amazing journey thus far and I feel like it is just beginning. I have come a long way in a short time and there are many people who have been there to help me along the way that I wish to thank for all their help and support.

First and foremost, I want to thank my family for their patience, encouragement and understanding. Thanks to my husband, Greg, for his support and for always cooking his wonderful meals for me while I am busy working in my studio. And thanks to my children, Brian and Michelle, for all their help and support and for becoming my greatest works of art. Thanks, Michelle, for your wonderful editing skills and all the help you have given me with the book and my quilting business. Thanks to my mom for introducing me to her sewing machine when I was a little girl and to both my parents, Rose and Joe Miller, for all the love and support they have always given me. Thanks to my brother, Lee Miller, for all his advice and encouragement and to my brother, Warren, for all his prayers.

There are many people in the sewing and quilting world who have helped and supported me on this journey that I wish to thank. A special thanks to Laura Haynie for recognizing my passion for sewing and recruiting me to become a Creative Consultant for Pfaff Sewing Machine and for all that she taught me. Thanks to Lurline Saint-George, who taught me to sew, so many years ago. Thanks to Theresa Robinson for all her support and for encouraging me to create and market my quilting products, And thanks to all the people at Pfaff Sewing Machine and VSM sewing who have been so wonderful to work with over the last few years.

There are many friends that I wish to thank for their support, advice and encouragement: Flo Barry, Nadine Mercader, Phyllis Taylor, Barbara Campbell and Yolanda Fundora, Aurelia May, Sandy Hammons, and all my wonderful friends from the Dallas Area Fiber Artists.

Thanks to everyone at Blank Textiles for making my fabric visions a reality. And thanks especially to Diana Mancini, for helping turn my design ideas into such beautiful fabrics to create these quilts.

A special thanks goes to Becky Harness, who was always willing to help me, at the last minute, by quilting my quilts when I ran out of time. She always put in the extra time and effort and skills to make sure that the quilting was beautiful and something special. All the quilts along the bottom of this page were quilted by Becky. Information about her quilting services can be found in the resource list at the end of the book.

Last but not least, I want to thank all the wonderful people at Krause Publications. Thanks to Andy Belmas, my editor, who has been a pleasure to work with. And thanks to Candy Wiza, Katie Newby, Bob Best and Kris Kandler for their help creating *Spinning Pinwheel Quilts.*

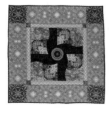    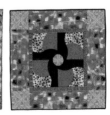 

Contents

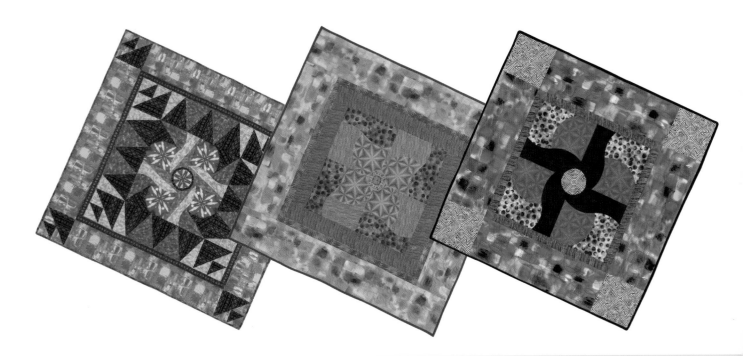

The 3-6-9 Design System™

The **3-6-9 Design System™** from SEW INSPIRED was created using only 9" blocks such as the Spinning Pinwheel block. All the designs that I have created can be easily combined in quilts because they all have common seam positions on the 3", 6" and 9" point in the blocks. There are three different curved 3-6-9 block designs available as components of the **3-6-9 Design System™**. Each of the three design kits include acrylic templates and a CD.

Spinning Pinwheel Block Design Kit

Winding Curve Block Design Kit

Spinning Fans Block Design Kit

Originally, I was going to write this book on the complete **3-6-9 Design System**™ consisting of all three of the blocks. However, once I got started, I realized there was enough information and design capabilities in each one to create three separate books. This book will focus on the Spinning Pinwheel quilts, the 3-6-9 Basic Building blocks and all you can create with them. You can find more information on the other **3-6-9 Design Systems**™ kits on my web site, www.sewinspired.com.

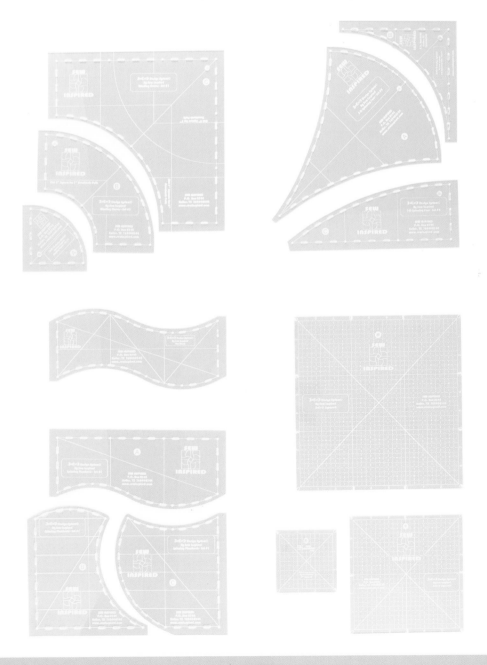

- - Understanding the 3-6-9 Design System™ - -

When you design a quilt using the **3-6-9 Design System™** by SEW INSPIRED, your creative possibilities are endless.

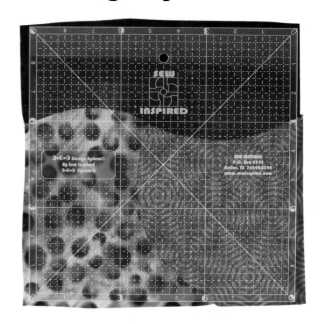

1. The finished block in your quilt will always be 9". This mean that the pieced block must be an accurate 9½" before it is sewn into your quilt.

2. All the seams in each block will always end on a 3", 6" or 9" position in your block. The illustration to the right shows a Spinning Pinwheel block that has a **3-6-9 Square-it Tool™** overlaid on top. As you can see, each seam line falls either on the 3", 6" or 9" marking of the ruler.

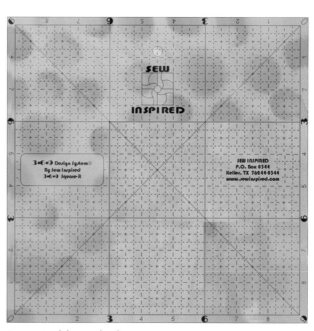

Basic Building Block

3. In this book, there are several variations of curved Spinning Pinwheel blocks and there are several variations of Basic Building Blocks. Like the curved blocks, the Basic Building Block seams always line up on the 0, 3", 6" or 9" points.

4. You can create any 9" block by piecing a combination of 6" and 3" squares and 3" x 6" or 3" x 9" rectangles (or combinations such as half squares or quarter square triangles). Below are examples of block configurations that all equal a finished 9" block.

5. Using like fabrics on pieces that share a 3", 6" or 9" inch seam point, you can create completely new designs because of the blending effect that occurs at those seam lines. Below is an example of two identical designs that look very different because like-colored fabrics are used on pieces that share 3", 6" or 9" seam points on the blocks.

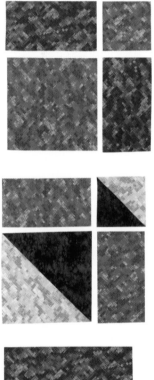

NOTE

See the Building Block Key on page 121 for examples of other blocks that you can create with these 3-6-9 units.

- - Designing Quilts Using the 3-6-9 Design System - -

On page 120 you will find the **3-6-9 Design System™** Block Key, which is the key to simple, easy, and unlimited design possibilities for Spinning Pinwheel quilt designs. Later in the book I will teach you how the blocks are constructed. Then we will use these blocks in all the projects and in the block charts that are included on the CD-ROM.

- - Rotating Blocks - -

A block will look completely different when you rotate it different ways. Below are four Spinning Pinwheel quilts that use the same blocks–they are simply rotated in different ways. Notice how different quilts look when the same blocks are turned in different directions.

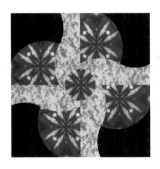 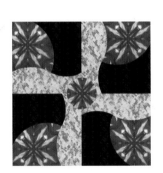 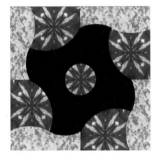 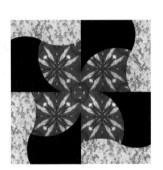

- - Planning Your Quilts - -

Since there are so many ways to put a Spinning Pinwheel design together, I suggest you start with a plan using the Spinning Pinwheel coloring book sheets found on the CD in the back of this book. There are four coloring book drawings of quilt designs you can make using the Spinning Pinwheel templates. Print out some designs that you like, and try coloring them with colored pencils, crayons or watercolors.

Once you have colored a design from the coloring book, you can use the Fabric Estimator Chart in the back of the book to estimate how much fabric you need.

HINT

Many times I have started with a plan only to change the design by rotating and rearranging the blocks. There is nothing wrong with changing your mind about the quilt you are working on. Once you get your blocks done, you may decide you like a different arrangement than your original design.

Getting Started

The templates for the Spinning Pinwheel blocks are asymmetrical, which can create a unique challenge for many quilters. Most quilting designs are completely symmetrical, so the block pieces are the same shape whether they are facing up or down. Since all the pieces of the Spinning Pinwheel blocks are asymmetrical, you must be consistent in the direction that your fabric and your templates face when you cut out the pieces of the block.

HINTS

Throughout this book you will always be using a ¼" seam allowance and will always place the right sides of your fabric together while sewing.

When cutting your pieces, make sure every layer of fabric is right-side up, and make sure the template is facing up (so you can read the writing). No matter how many times I've said this in my classes, there is always someone who cuts half the pieces backwards.

If you use a batik or some hand-dyed fabrics, you don't have to worry about which way your fabric faces when you cut out your templates, since most of these fabrics are the same on both sides.

TOOLS OF THE TRADE
- - Sewing Machine - -

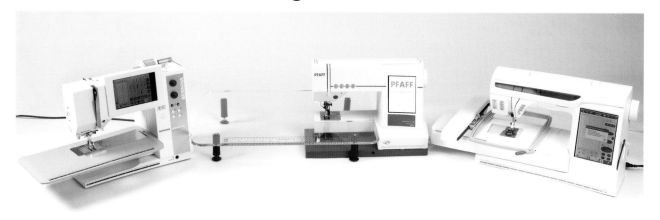

My recommendation for selecting the right sewing machine is to buy the best machine that you can afford and, most importantly, buy it from a sewing machine dealer that offers outstanding support. It is so important to work with a dealer who will train you on the machine operations and who will offer creative classes that will let you get the most out of your machine. There are lots of wonderful sewing machines on the market that can do some amazing things, but if you never learn how to use that machine to its fullest potential, then you will be wasting your money. If you get frustrated because your machine doesn't work the way you expect it to, quilting won't be any fun.

One of the machine features I use most is the needle-up/needle-down button. This button allows your machine to keep the needle in the down position whenever you stop sewing. Stopping with the needle embedded in the fabric makes it easy to pivot around curves and is helpful when you are doing machine appliqué. Some machines can even automatically raise the presser foot while keeping the needle in the down position, and lower the presser foot again automatically when you resume sewing. This is a feature that I can't live without! It holds your fabric in place with the needle, but lets you easily pivot the fabric while you are sewing around the curves, so you don't have to keep taking your hands off the fabric to raise and lower your presser foot. A knee lift will also work well for sewing curves, since it allows you to keep your hands on the fabric while you are raising and lowering the presser foot with your knee.

- - Presser Feet - -

Using the right foot for the job will make all the difference in the world in your piecing and quilting. There are many specialty feet for all the sewing machines on the market today, but a few are absolutely essential for quilting and will help to make your quilting fun and easy.

¼" Foot: This foot is essential for accurate piecing. Some sewing machine manufacturers have a ¼" foot with an edge guide. It is a wonderful foot if it is available for your machine.

Open-Toe Foot: This is the perfect foot for decorative stitching and machine appliqué. An open-toe foot lets you see very clearly where your stitches are going on your fabric.

Open-Toe Quilting or Darning Foot: Having an open-toe quilting foot will help you get your quilting stitches where you want them because you will have a clearer view of where you are going.

Piping or Narrow Cording Foot: This foot is very helpful if you plan on inserting piping in the binding of your quilt, which is one of my favorite binding treatments.

Walking Foot or Even-Feed Foot: A walking foot (integrated on your machine or removable) is essential for good quality quilting and piecing.

Straight-Stitch Needle Plate: I always use a single needle plate on my machine when machine piecing. It improves the quality of my stitches and prevents the beginning edge of the fabric from being forced down into the bobbin case, which can happen if you are using a throat-plate for zig-zag stitching. A straight-stitch needle plate has a very small circular opening and can only be used when you are sewing a straight stitch.

- - Sewing Machine Needles - -

I have found the best needle for piecing is either a Topstitch 80/12 or a 70/11. I will usually decide on the needle based on the fabric and thread. I use a Topstitch needle for almost all my quilting. Microtex Sharps and Jeans needles are excellent for very tightly woven fabrics like batiks. The most important thing to remember is to change your needle at the beginning of every new project.

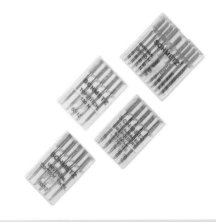

- - Design Walls and Surfaces - -

A design wall (or similar surface) is an essential tool for creating and evaluating your quilt designs. Not everyone has the space to install a true design wall, so there are lots of ways to improvise. For a quick-and-easy portable design wall, sew two pieces of white flannel together, and tape or tack them to a blank wall. If you do have a sewing room with space for a permanent design wall, you can make one with insulation boards purchased at a hardware store. Pad them with batting

HINT

If you don't have an empty wall, look for a folding room divider that you can pad and cover with flannel and put in a closet when you aren't using it.

and cover with white flannel. Using a design wall made from flannel lets you easily move around blocks and then stand away to evaluate the design from a distance.

- - Rotary Cutter, Mats and Rulers - -

There are lots of different rotary cutters, mats and rulers on the market. When selecting a rotary cutter, look for one that feels comfortable in your hand and one that has a safety locking mechanism. I like the kind that automatically retracts when you aren't using it. A 28-mm rotary cutter is best for cutting curves. If you try to cut curved templates with a blade larger than 28 mm, you will nick your blade when going around the curves and will have to replace it often. If you have trouble with arthritis or carpal tunnel, look for ergonomic rotary cutters that are great for straight rotary cutting.

When selecting a mat, look for one that is easily readable and self healing. Two-

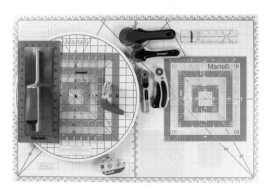

sided mats last twice as long since you can flip them over when one side gets worn out.

There are tons of rulers on the market. I recommend you use rulers that have very fine lines that will show up against most fabrics and that you can comfortably see.

- - Scissors and Snips - -

Make sure your scissors stay sharp. Use your fabric scissors for fabric only; use separate scissors for cutting plastic templates and paper. You should also have small snips or sharp embroidery scissors in addition to larger, sharp scissors.

- - Basting Tape and Pins - -

For piecing, I like to use very long, fine pins. For pin basting my quilts, I use curved #2 quilting pins.

Wash-A-Way Wonder Tape™ from W.H. Collins is a two-sided water soluble tape that is the key to the Sew Inspired **E-Z Pinless Piecing Method™**. Wonder tape is a ¼" tape that will dissolve in water. It is extremely sticky and takes some practice, but once you get the hang of it, it will become your best friend!

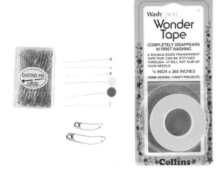

- - Threads - -

Buy high quality thread! Cheap thread will cause problems with your sewing machine and create thread-tension problems. Check with thread company Web sites for recommended needles to use with each type of thread. (See resource directory on page 126 for thread companies).

Piecing: 50-weight cotton top and bobbin thread used with an 80/12 topstitch needle.
Quilting: Any thread your machine will comfortably use. When using cotton, I prefer 30- or 40-weight.

Quilting and Embellishing
Metallic thread: All metallic threads can be used for top and bobbin thread.
Flat metallic thread: I prefer Superior's Glitter and Sulky Holoshimmer
Rayon thread: I prefer 30- or 40-weight rayon thread.

HINT

The embellishment threads listed here are also great for embroidery and other special embellishments.

When using metallic thread, loosen the upper tension on your machine to 1 and use a 90/14 topstitch needle.

- - Pressing Supplies - -

A good steam iron can be a quilter's best friend. Steam and starch will flatten just about any seams (even curved seams) if done properly. My recommendation is to buy the best iron you can afford. A good iron will last a long time, produces lots of steam and is well worth the money. An iron with a separate reservoir gives greater steam and you don't have to constantly refill it.

Starch is an essential for quilting curved seams. With starch and steam, you can get any block to lay flat. For curved piecing, be sure your fabric is stabilized with starch before you cut the pieces. As you will learn later, you will be working with bias edges that can stretch very easily. Starch will hold those edges and let them stretch only when you want them to.

Iron cleaning gels work very effectively when the sole-plate of your iron gets gunked up with starch. Placing a press cloth over the fabric after you spray on the starch can prevent some "gunkiness." Nevertheless, the iron will need to be cleaned periodically.

HINT Automatic shut-off irons are great if you are forgetful, but can be very frustrating if you spend a lot of time quilting and need to have your iron hot and ready to use at a moment's notice. Just be sure to turn the iron off when you are done for the day.

HINT A used dryer sheet works well to clean the iron if it hasn't gotten too dirty.

- - Ergonomics and Quilting - -

The repetitive motions of sewing and quilting can cause stress to your neck, back, arms and hands. Tools, tables and chairs (and your posture) play important roles in your comfort and success.

A flat surface is essential for free-motion quilting. A good piece of furniture that is designed for sewing and quilting is well worth the money. My quilting table was one of the best investments I've ever made, next to purchasing the best sewing machine I could afford. The bills from my chiropractor dropped dramatically once I started using a proper sewing table.

Some tips that I can give you based on my own experience to prevent injuries while quilting are:

Take breaks often: Limit sewing and quilting to an hour and then take a break.

Keep a set of light hand weights under your sewing table: If you feel tension in you neck, shoulders or arms, grab your weights and exercise for five minutes. Exercising and stretching helps prevent injuries and will give you more energy.

Make sure that your chair is at the proper height for your sewing table: Your elbows should be at a right angle when placed on top of the bed of your machine, and you should be able to hold your shoulders in a relaxed position while you are sewing.

Pay attention to your posture while sewing: Slumping over your machine will cause stress to your neck and back.

Fabric and Color Theory

A quilt can be pieced and quilted perfectly, but if you don't select fabrics that work with your design in the right colors, you may not be happy with your results. In this chapter, we will explore the role of color, value and scale in making choices about fabric and design.

- - Fabric Scale - -

Fabric scale is the size of the pattern design or repeat. There is a tremendous variety of fabric scale to choose from, but be careful selecting fabrics to use together. Quilters have a tendency to shy away from large-scale designs in fabric because they don't know how to use them. However, a well-selected large-print fabric can become the main design focus of your quilt. This technique can be very effective if you select the fabric well, or it can ruin your design if the fabric doesn't play well with its neighbors. Below are two identical blocks of similar colors that demonstrate what happens

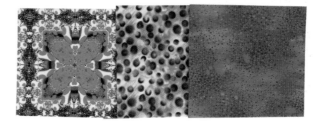

with different fabric scales. The first block uses large-scale dots; the second block uses small-scale dots. As you can see from these blocks, the large dots detract from the shapes that are clearly visible in the small-dot print block.

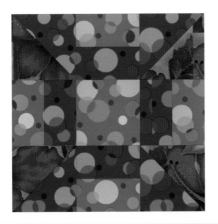

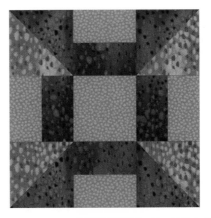

- - The Color Wheel - -

Red, yellow and blue are the primary colors. If you mix primary colors, you get secondary colors. Mixing red and blue gives you violet; mixing yellow and blue makes green; mixing yellow and red results in orange. Tertiary colors are blue-violet, red-violet, red-orange, yellow-orange, yellow-green and blue-green. Tertiary colors are made by mixing primary and secondary colors that are adjacent on the color wheel.

Shade, tint and tone are terms that refer to the amount of black, white or gray that is added to a color. Tint is the addition of white to create a lighter color. Shade is the addition of black to create a darker color. Tone is the addition of gray to dull down a color.

- - Value - -

One of the most important aspects of color in quilt-making is value. Value refers to how light or dark your fabric is in relation to the other fabrics in your quilt. In the blocks below, the design is much more prominent in the block on the right because there is so much more contrast between the color values. If you squint your eyes and a design element seems to disappear, you probably don't have enough contrast between the fabric as is the case for the block on the left.

When selecting fabric for your Spinning Pinwheel quilts, value is probably the most important aspect of the color selection process. An interesting aspect of value in quilting is that it is all relative to the other fabrics that you are using. One fabric can be a light fabric in one quilt and a dark in another. The picture below shows a fabric that is a dark value in the first group and then becomes a light value in the second group.

If you want a distinctly visible pinwheel effect, the pieces that make up the Spinning Pinwheel blocks should be substantially different in value. On the right are two quilt designs that demonstrate how important value is to the design of the quilt. Quilt A shows a very distinct design because of the value differences of each piece in the block. Quilt B, which is the exact same quilt design, uses colors that have the same value, giving it much less impact and interest.

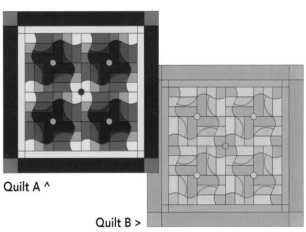

Quilt A ^

Quilt B >

There are a few simple tricks to selecting fabrics based on value. If you aren't sure if there is enough value contrast, lay your fabric candidates down, step about four feet away, take off your glasses (if you wear them) and look at them through squinted eyes. You can see the value differences better if the fabrics are blurred. You can also check your fabric's relative value by making black-and-white copies. Removing color makes the true value of a fabric more obvious, especially when the fabric has multiple colors with varying values. The same effect can be achieved with a digital camera set to monochrome mode. This is my favorite method to check value and contrast between the quilt elements.

Color intensity refers to how pure a color is. Highly intense colors, such as those seen on a color wheel, are the purest colors and will appear very bright and cheery when used in your quilts. Low intensity colors make a more subtle, subdued and quieter quilt. As you can see from the quilts in this book, I don't make dull quilts. I love color, and the brighter the better! Color intensity is purely a matter of personal taste. If you like your quilts to have a more subdued feel, you should look for fabric with colors that have been dulled.

- - Selecting Color - -

My students often want to know how to select their color combinations. Some people are very good at this part of the design process and there are many who are admittedly "color challenged." If you are one of those color-challenged quilters, my recommendation is to look to the professionals for color inspiration. Also, I recommend that you keep a color scrapbook for ideas about color. Your scrapbook can be an actual scrapbook or a digital one if you have a digital camera and a computer. Here are some of the places you can look for color ideas and inspiration and pictures for your scrapbook:

Master artists: Study work by Van Gogh, Picasso, Monet and others at museums or in art books. These artists know color that works, so why not take advantage of their skills and knowledge?

Advertising in magazines: Advertising agencies use talented artists to create their advertising, and color plays a big part in the appeal of all advertising.

Quilt shows: There is nothing wrong with creating a quilt using a color scheme you loved in someone else's quilt. You aren't copying the quilt, just getting your color inspiration from it.

Fashion designers: If you see a dress that you absolutely love because of the colors, snap a picture with a digital camera for your color scrapbook.

Nature: Sunsets, flowers, animals, seashells, rocks and mountains are all sources for color ideas. The most natural color schemes will come from nature.

Product packaging: Skilled artists create packaging with appealing colors.

Fabric designers: Look at the color dots on the selvage of your favorite fabrics, and create a quilt with the same color scheme. (You don't necessarily even need to use that fabric in the quilt, just the colors in it.)

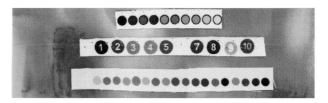

Model homes: Model homes are often decorated by professional interior designers. The colors used by these designers can be an excellent source for design ideas in quilts.

- - Quality Fabric - -

The best way to tell if a fabric is high quality is by the weave and the feel of the fabric. The weave should be very tight. If you hold the fabric up to the light and you can see through it very clearly because it is loosely woven, don't buy it. You don't want to spend all your precious time on a quilt that won't survive over time.

"Feel" is another factor when purchasing a fabric. Low-quality fabric that has a loose weave will often feel very stiff, because the manufacturer has added a lot of fabric sizing to give it more body. If it feels stiff, it is usually low quality. One exception is batik fabrics. Many high-quality batiks are very tightly woven, which can make them feel stiffer than other fabrics. I can always tell a high-quality fabric by its feel. It should have a good "hand," which means that it should feel soft but still sturdy and should drape well.

- - Fabric Preparation - -

Is it necessary to wash your fabric before you start your quilts? The "Quilt Police" will tell you that you should always wash your fabric before you start your project. I have to admit, I have never been great at following rules – the "washing rule" is one that I have never obeyed. My feeling about prewashing fabric is that it is too time consuming and in most instances unnecessary. There are exceptions. Most of the quilts I make are art quilts that will hang on a wall, and I don't believe in putting art into a washing machine. However, if you are making a bed quilt that will be repeatedly washed, you may want to prewash your fabric. I have found that if you buy high-quality fabric from a reputable quilt shop, you will not have problems with colorfastness or shrinkage.

While I don't pre-wash my fabric, I do occasionally pre-test a small piece of fabric if I suspect it could be troublesome. The fabrics that I usually pre-test are reds, yellows and all hand-dyed fabrics. To pre-test fabric, cut out a four-inch square, and place it on top of a piece of white fabric in the sink. Run hot water over the fabric, and let it sit in the sink for 15-20 minutes. Check to see if any color came off onto the white fabric. You can further test the colorfastness by rubbing the wet colored fabric against the wet white fabric. If the color doesn't run, then it won't run when you wash your quilt after it's finished.

ALL ABOUT TEMPLATES

Due to the curved shapes used to make the Spinning Pinwheel block, it is necessary to use templates to cut out your fabric pieces. Since making templates is time consuming and we would all rather spend that time quilting, I decided to have the templates for my Spinning Pinwheel quilts commercially manufactured and available as the **Sew Inspired 3-6-9 Design System™**. I have designed the Spinning Pinwheel templates so that you will be able to get a perfect block every time when you square up the blocks using the **3-6-9 Square-it Tool™**, a squaring ruler specifically designed for the **Sew Inspired 3-6-9 Design System templates™**. Using commercially designed acrylic templates is easier, more accurate, and certainly much more convenient than making your own templates. However, since there may be some quilters who would like to make their own templates out of flexible plastic, this chapter will show how to make your own templates and how to use the **Sew Inspired 3-6-9 Design System™** acrylic templates.

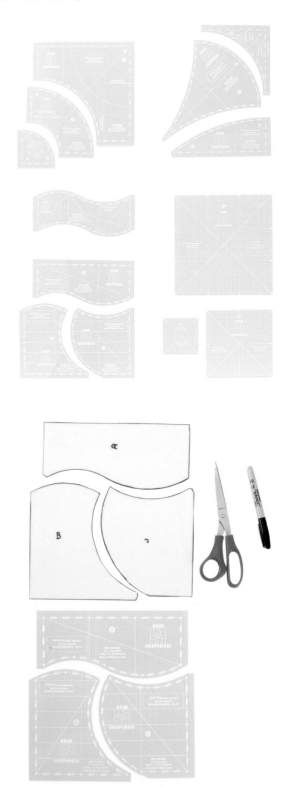

MAKING YOUR OWN TEMPLATES

Step 1
Insert the enclosed CD into your computer. Print out template pieces A, B and C on your computer printer.

Step 2
Tape each printed template to a piece of the Mylar template sheet. Trace the outside outline of the templates onto the plastic template sheet using your thin permanent black marker, as shown in the picture below.

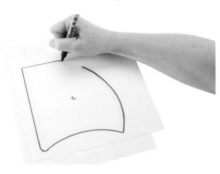

Step 3
Mark the corner dots shown on each of the template pieces with your permanent black marker.

Step 4
Trace all the other lines shown on the paper template pattern onto your plastic template using a straight edge as a guide.

Step 5
Using your X-ACTO knife or sharp scissors, cut out the three template pieces. Make sure your cut edges are smooth curves, and follow your drawn lines precisely.

MATERIALS

Mylar template sheet
X-ACTO knife or sharp scissors
Thin permanent black marker
Computer and printer
Small hole punch or sharp stiletto
Double-sided scotch tape

Step 6
Using a hole punch or sharp stiletto, punch out all the corner dot marks. Make the hole large enough to fit a pencil tip through.

Step 7
Place a few pieces of double-sided tape on the underside of your cut-out templates to help hold them in place once you start cutting your fabric.

Step 8
Using your permanent marker, write "right side" on the top of your templates. Since this is an asymmetrical design, you must always cut the pieces so that the right side of the template is facing up and ALL layers of your fabric must also be right side up. You won't be able to put the block together correctly if you cut any layers with the fabric's right side facing down.

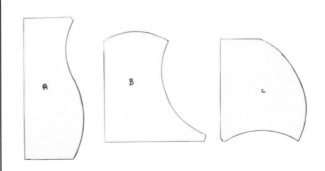

USING THE 3-6-9 DESIGN SYSTEM™ TEMPLATES
- - Curved Piecing and the "Ease-factor" - -

Below is a picture of the SEW INSPIRED 3-6-9 Design System Spinning Pinwheel acrylic templates.

The design of these templates is unique in that I have added what I refer to as the **3-6-9 Fudge-Factor™**. After making hundreds of blocks containing curved seams and constantly finding that the blocks ended up smaller than they should have been, I realized that it wasn't a result of careless sewing, but the result of the ease-factor.

When you sew two curved seams together, it is necessary to ease one curve into the other, because – due to bias edges – the two curves will be slightly different. This is the reason that blocks with curved seams always seem to shrink when you piece them. To compensate for this "ease-factor," I have made the outside straight edges of my acrylic templates slightly larger than they need to be so that the blocks will all end up being too large rather than too small after they are pieced. A block that is too large can be easily trimmed down, but you can't add fabric back on (seamlessly at least) to fix a block that ends up too small.

Since I have only added the extra 3-6-9 Fudge-Factor to the outside straight edges of the templates, there will be no change to the curved seams in the blocks and they will still end up on the 3", 6" or 9" point on the block. Once you have pieced your block together, you can trim the block down to exactly 9½" using the specially designed **SEW INSPIRED 3-6-9 Square-It Tool™**. Just line up your seams on the 3" or 6" mark on the ruler, as shown in the picture below.

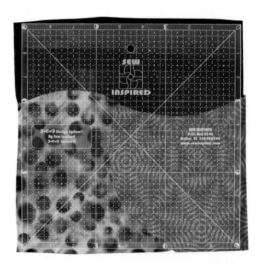

- - The Basics of Rotary Cutting and Using Acrylic Templates - -

Using acrylic templates allows much more creativity in your quilting since you can introduce many more unique shapes into your quilts. You will need to learn some basics about rotary cutting with templates. It's important to understand that rotary cutters can be dangerous if not used properly. Make sure your blade is retracted when you set it down after using it. Always use a sharp blade. Dull blades do a poor job of cutting fabric and are very dangerous. Always cut on a rotary cutting mat. Self-healing mats are much better to use, as they last longer and tend to keep your blades sharper much longer.

When cutting curves, it is important to use a 28-mm rotary cutter. The smaller 28-mm blades will go around the inside curves much easier than the larger 45-mm blades. You won't be as likely to nick your blade against the template plastic with smaller blades. You can cut up to four layers of fabric quite easily with a 28-mm rotary cutter. A 45-mm blade works well when you are cutting any straight strips or pieces. A 6" x 24" straight, clear acrylic rotary cutting ruler is one of my most used rulers because it allows me to cut completely across the width of most quilting fabrics, which are usually around 22" wide when folded as it comes off the bolt.

When cutting your fabric pieces with a rotary cutter and templates, always cut away from your body. Cut on the corner of your cutting table so you can walk around the table to cut the other side of the template piece, rather than cutting towards your body. I like to cut my templates on a smaller mat. I can turn the mat, leaving my fabric and templates in place so that I can always cut away from my body. Turntable cutting mats are very good for cutting fabrics using templates.

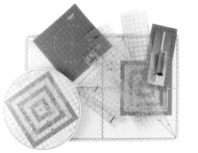

HINTS

Use an automatically retractable rotary cutter, so you don't have to retract it when you're done using it.

Double-sided tape helps keep templates in place when you are cutting. Replace the tape periodically because lint causes it to lose its stickiness.

When cutting with templates, place your little finger just off the edge of the template to make sure that the template doesn't shift while cutting.

CURVED PIECING THE E-Z WAY

Since there are many different ways to approach piecing, I have found it's best to show students all the possible ways to accomplish a task, and then let them determine their preferred method. For this reason, I will demonstrate the two different curved piecing methods I use, and you can decide which one you like using best. I encourage you to try them both on curved-seam blocks before you decide which one you like best.

There are two curved piecing construction methods discussed in this section:

• The Pinless E-Z Curve Piecing Method
• The Pinless Edge Matching Method

The Pinless E-Z Curve Piecing Method is the best method for a beginning quilter who has not had much experience with curved seams. This method uses a water-soluble double-sided tape called Wonder-Tape by Collins instead of pins. The advantage of this method is that you will ease the block pieces together before you ever sew a stitch into them. This method takes a bit more time up front, but it will save you time in the long run because you won't be spending any time "un-sewing" seams that didn't come out perfectly. With this method, you will make sure that all your seams lie perfectly flat and are pucker-free before you actually sew them. This chapter focuses on constructing the block; all subsequent chapters will show you the many different ways to use this wonderful block.

THE PINLESS E-Z CURVED PIECING METHOD

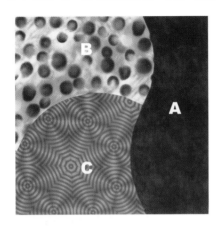

The Spinning Pinwheel block is a simple 9" (finished) block that consist of three template pieces, which are labeled and shown in the diagram above. You must sew Pieces C and B together before you can attach Piece A.

Step 1
With a water-soluble marker or pencil, mark through the corner point holes of your template pieces onto the right sides of your fabrics so that you will be able to accurately match your end pieces together.

Step 2
Affix the end of the tape to one of the end points on Piece C that you marked in Step 1.

HINT

When using Wonder Tape for piecing, I always apply the tape to the "hill" or convex side of the curve rather than the "valley" or concave side.

Step 3
Roll out a segment of Wonder Tape that will reach the other marked dot.

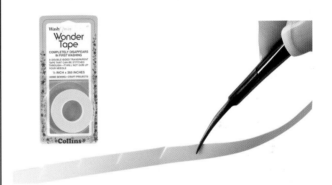

Step 4
Once the tape is rolled out, use a scissors to snip about two thirds of the way through the tape at 1" intervals so that you will be able to apply the tape around the curve. (Cut at an angle as shown.)

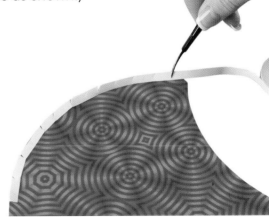

Step 5

Stick the tape to the right-side curved edge of Piece C between the two dots you marked in Step 1 as shown.

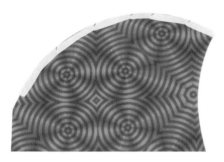

Step 6

Just before you are ready to match Pieces B and C together, peel the paper from the top of the Wonder Tape that you have just attached to Piece C.

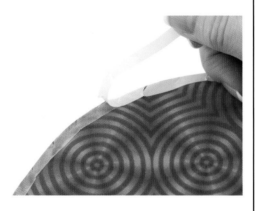

Step 7

With right sides together, match the end points you marked in Step 2 on Pieces B and C as shown.

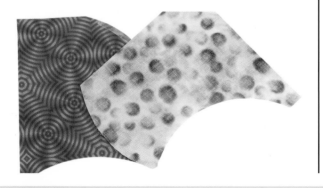

Step 8

After Pieces B and C are stuck together at the end points, press the fabric edges together with your fingers. Begin at the end points and work towards the middle until you have matched your edges all the way to the center.

HINT

Your edges should match up together perfectly flat without any puckers.

When taping B and C together, you may find that you have more fabric on one side than the other, and it will look like the pieces will never match up properly. If this happens, just release the section that seems too small and slightly stretch the edge until the two edges are perfectly aligned. You may have to do this in a few spots around the curve if you can't stretch one section enough. It works every time if you've cut your pieces accurately. This is where working on the bias edges becomes a big advantage.

If you don't get your pieces matched perfectly the first time, you can also pull apart the two sides completely and re-stick them together until you have the pieces lined up perfectly. That's the beauty of this method, you can make sure your pieces will go together perfectly before you ever sew them.

Step 9

When Piece B and C are taped together, open them up and make sure the pieces will lay flat. If the pieces look good when opened, stitch them together with a ¼" seam allowance using a ¼" foot.

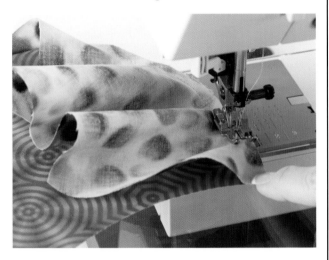

HINT

To sew around the curve, stitch slowly and raise your presser foot with your needle down to pivot around the curve.

Step 10

To attach Piece A to Piece BC, apply Wonder Tape to the right side curves of BC as shown. (See Steps 3 - 5.) Remove the paper from the Wonder Tape.

Step 11

With right sides together, match the end points of Piece BC to the right side of Piece A as shown.

Step 12

Repeat Steps 7 and 8 by matching the center point and the two end points. Starting at both end points and working your way to the middle, finger press the fabrics together just as you did with Pieces B and C.

Step 13

Check that your pieces are taped together perfectly flat with no puckers. Using a ¼" foot, sew them together with a ¼" seam allowance.

Congratulations! You have just completed your first block. Now that you know the Pinless E-Z Curve Piecing Method, it's smooth sailing from here.

THE EDGE-MATCHING METHOD

The Pinless E-Z Curve Piecing Method is a fool-proof method, great for beginning to intermediate quilters. Once you are skilled at this method for piecing curved seams, you might want to try another pinless curved piecing method called the Edge-Matching Method. With practice, this method works very well, but there is a greater likelihood of pieces not matching up perfectly. If you are using the green SEW INSPIRED Spinning Pinwheel acrylic templates, I have added what I call the extra "Fudge Factor," which creates a slightly oversized 9½" block, so any uneven edges will get cut off when you square up your blocks.

Step 1

As in the previous method, you will piece B and C together first. With this method, there is no pinning or tape. You must first match up the top right hand corners of pieces B and C as shown.

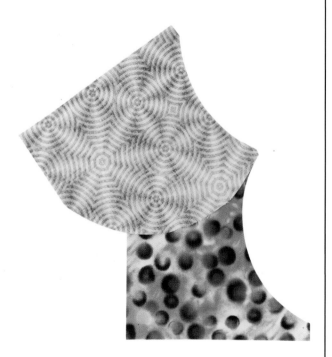

Step 2

Place the two matched corners under the presser foot with piece C on top of piece B and start sewing at the fabric edge as shown.

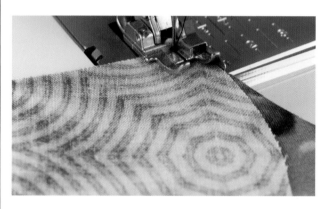

HINT

If you have a needle-down function on your sewing machine, you want to engage it while you are sewing. If you don't have a needle-down function, manually put your needle down whenever you stop sewing. The needle-down position will hold your fabric in place while you pivot around the curves.

Step 3

Sew 2 or 3 stitches, and stop with the needle in the down position. Raise the presser foot, and gently pivot Piece C to match up to the edge of Piece B on the bottom layer.

Step 4

Sew 5 or 6 stitches, and stop with the needle down. Gently pull the edge of Piece C to match up to the edge of Piece B just in front of the presser foot. Be careful not to stretch your fabric.

HINT

The trick to easing a curve in fabric is to hold the top layer of fabric up as it goes under the presser foot, but making sure to keep your fabric edges aligned.

Step 5

Repeat Step 4 until you sew to the end of Piece B.

HINT

For beautifully-sewn blocks, stop often to realign the edges and sew slowly without pulling or stretching your fabric.

Step 6

Press the seams to one side.

HINT

If you have a very dark fabric, it is usually best to press the seams toward the dark fabric so that the seam allowances don't show through the lighter fabric.

Step 7

Place Piece A on top of Piece BC with top corner offset ¼" as shown.

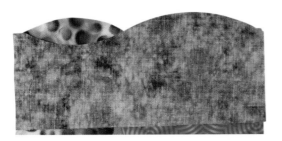

Step 8

Sew 5 or 6 stitches, and stop with the needle down. Gently pull the edge of Piece C to match up to the edge of Piece B just in front of the presser foot. Be careful not to stretch your fabric.

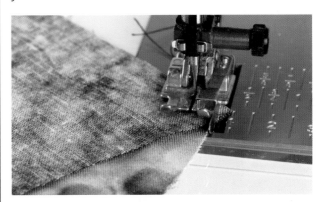

Step 9

Repeat all the above steps to complete all the Spinning Pinwheel blocks for your quilt.

Spinning Pinwheel Block Variations

It is truly amazing how many quilt designs can be derived from the basic Spinning Pinwheel block. With three curved pieces that each have seams that end on either the 3", 6" or 9" position of the block, you can easily mix and match other similarly designed blocks. You will have loads of fun playing with all the creative design possibilities of this unique, new block.

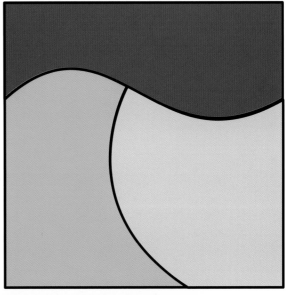

THE BASIC SPINNING PINWHEEL BLOCK

Below are the four 3-6-9 Spinning Pinwheel design configurations, made by using four basic Spinning Pinwheel blocks each turned a different way. The circles in the center of the four block configurations represent a circular appliqué that I often add to the 3-6-9 blocks to create a central focal point. Information on applying the center circular appliqués pictured in these diagrams can be found on page 116.

Spinning Pinwheels

Dogwood

Spinning Windmill

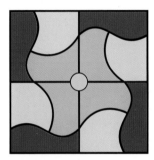

Spinning Feet

On the right are examples of quilt designs using only the basic Spinning Pinwheel block:

Quilt 6-1

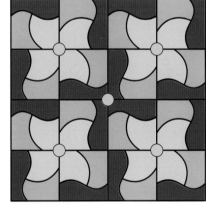

Quilt 6-2

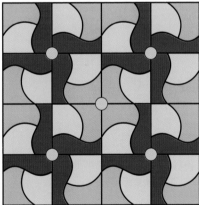

Quilt 6-3

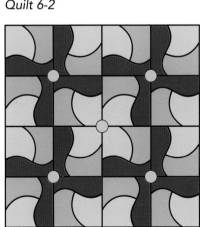

Quilt 6-4

When you combine four of the primary designs shown on the previous page, you will see a secondary design in the center of the quilt. In Quilt 6-1 there are four Spinning Pinwheel configurations put together, creating Spinning Feet as a secondary block design in the center. Quilt 6-2 is four Dogwood configurations, which forms a Spinning Windmill block in the center. Quilt 6-3 is four Spinning Feet configurations that form a Spinning Pinwheel in the Center and Quilt 6-4 consists of four Spinning Windmills, creating a Dogwood in the center. As you can see, turning the blocks in different directions results in many different quilt designs.

NOTE

The circles shown in many of the quilt diagrams represent circular appliqués that can be made with circular motif designs called Appliqué Printables which are printed on your home printer on inkjet fabric sheets. Several Appliqué Printables can be found on the CD in the back of this book.

The Spinning Pinwheel block seems like a very simple design, but the blocks can create all kinds of quilts, from traditional quilts to contemporary art quilts.

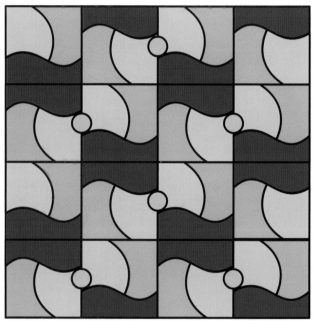

Quilt 6-5

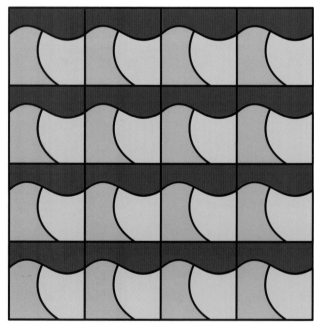

Quilt 6-6

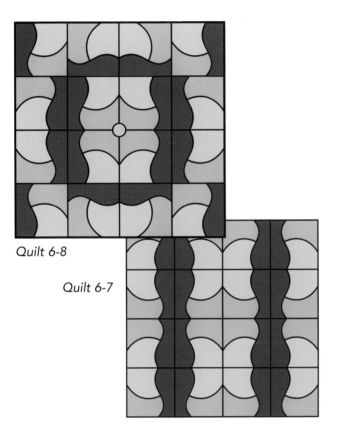

Quilt 6-8

Quilt 6-7

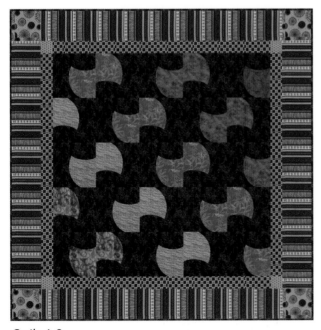

By simply changing the position and adding some circular appliqués, you can create a contemporary art quilt such as Quilt 6-5. Quilts 6-6, 6-7 and 6-8 are made using 16 basic Spinning Pinwheel blocks turned in different directions. Each of these quilts has a totally different look and feel. Once you have learned how to make the basic block, you can start designing all sorts of new and exciting quilts.

Every rule can be broken. To increase your design options, cut fabric layers with right sides together to create the mirror image blocks as shown in Quilt 6-7 and 6-8.

Block PW1

Quilt 6-9 shows an inventive design using the same brown background fabric for both Piece A and B with a change to the fabric color for Piece C. The basic Spinning Pinwheel block is the only block I've used in this quilt design.

Quilt 6-9

DIAGONAL SPLIT BLOCKS

By simply strip piecing fabrics together prior to cutting out the template shapes, you can create more intricate and complicated-looking designs with very little effort. Simply align the diagonal lines on your templates to the seam lines of pre-pieced fabric strips and then cut out your template shapes, and you have just eliminated many hours of potentially difficult piecing. This is an easy piecing method that lets even a beginner look like a pro! There are diagonal lines engraved on the templates that can open a whole new avenue to your creativity. If you make your own templates, you can add these diagonal lines as well. This chapter will show you all the different combinations of blocks that can be made using this piecing technique, as well as how to construct the various diagonally split blocks. Block labels on the Spinning Pinwheel Block Key on the next page will be referred to throughout the book and on the CD in the various project instruction and project sheets.

Split designs are a very easy way to create very complex and unique looking quilts without all the work of piecing difficult seams. This section will show you all the different combinations of diagonal split blocks that you can make to create unlimited numbers of 3-6-9 quilt designs.

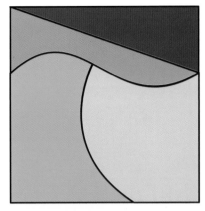

DS1

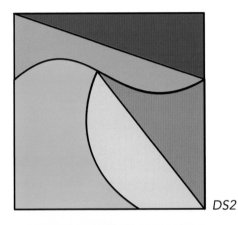

DS2

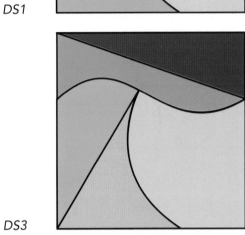

DS3

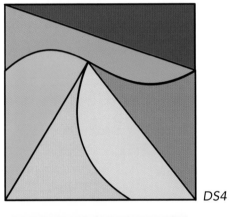

DS4

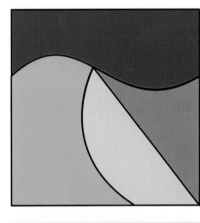

DS5

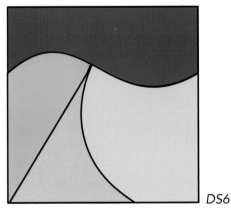

DS6

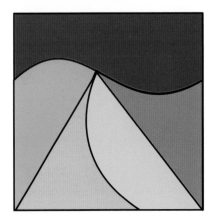

DS7

- - Single Diagonal Split Piece A Block - -

Step 1
Cut two strips of fabric 5" wide by the width of fabric.

Step 2
Sew those two strips with right sides together using a ¼" seam allowance.

Step 3
Press open the seams using a fairly heavy dose of spray starch.

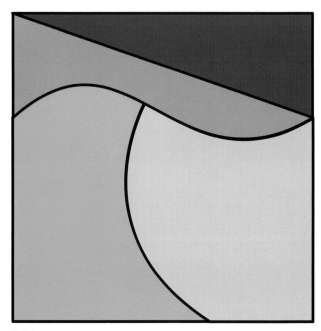

DS1

HINT
Any time you are making diagonal split blocks, the edges of your block will be on the bias and need a substantial amount of added stability. Use a substantial coating of spray starch or sizing.

Step 4
Line up your Piece A template so that the diagonal line on the template is directly over the seam line of the two piece strip sewn together in Step 2. Cut around the template using a 28-mm rotary cutter.

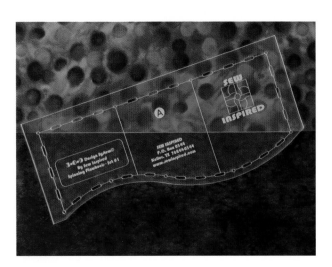

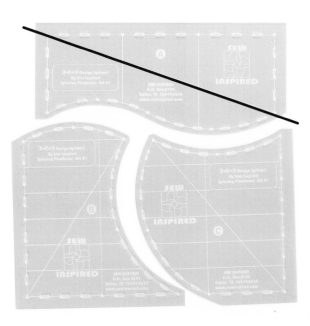

- - Single Diagonal Split Piece B Block - -

To create a diagonal split B block, line up your pieced seam on the diagonal line on Template B as shown.

Step 1
Cut two strips of fabric 6" wide by the width of fabric.

Step 2
Sew those two strips together with right sides together using a ¼" seam allowance.

Step 3
Press open your seams using a fairly heavy dose of spray starch.

Step 4
Line up your Piece B template so that the diagonal line on the template is directly over the seam line of the two pieces that you've just sewn together. Cut around the template using your 28-mm rotary cutter.

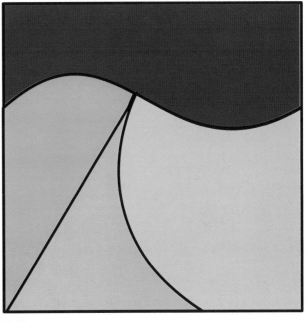

DS6

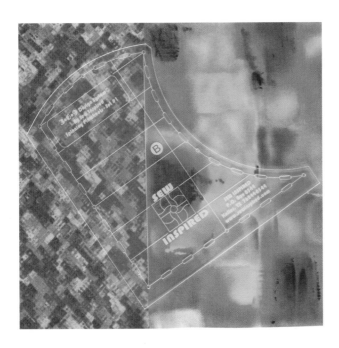

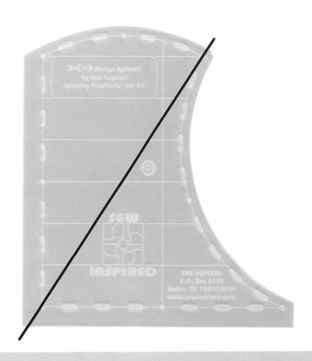

- - Single Diagonal Split Piece C Block - -

To create the single diagonal split block C, follow directions on page 38, but use Piece C template.

follow directions on page 38

HINT

You can cut four layers of fabric at the same time. Just make sure that you have all the seam lines precisely aligned before you cut your blocks and that all the fabric pieces are facing up.

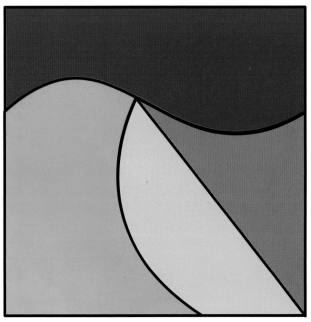

DS5

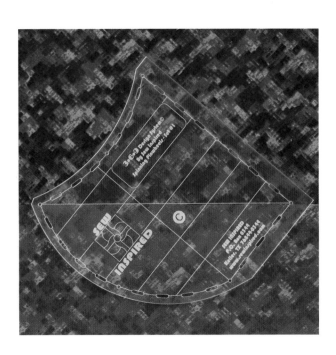

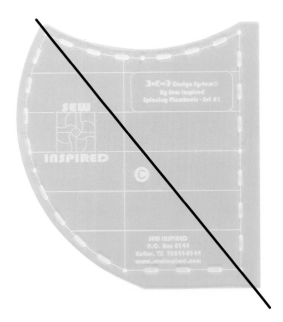

- - Double Diagonal Split Pieces BC and AC - -

To create a double diagonal split block with pieces B and C split, follow the directions to split each piece as described above on the single split block and piece together your pinwheel block as described on page 26. You can also create quilts splitting Pieces A and C or A and B as shown.

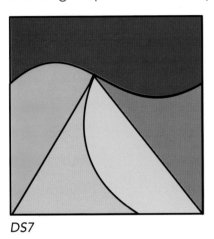

DS7

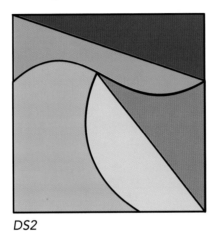

DS2

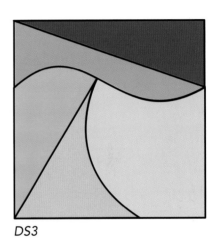

DS3

- - Triple Diagonal Split ABC - -

Below is a diagram of the triple diagonal split block that has all three pieces split diagonally. Don't forget that if you are making these split designs, it is extremely important to heavily starch your blocks since they will all have bias edges.

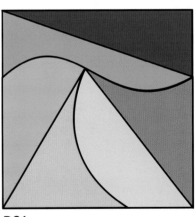

DS4

VERTICAL SPLIT BLOCKS

In this chapter I will show the creative possibilities of using the vertical split design. Vertical lines on the SEW INSPIRED Spinning Pinwheel templates let you strip piece fabric together prior to rotary cutting to create the vertical split block. These lines can be drawn on templates that you have made as well. On the following page is the Vertical Split Block Key showing all the different ways to create Vertical Split Blocks, which will be referred to when making projects that use Vertical Split Designs.

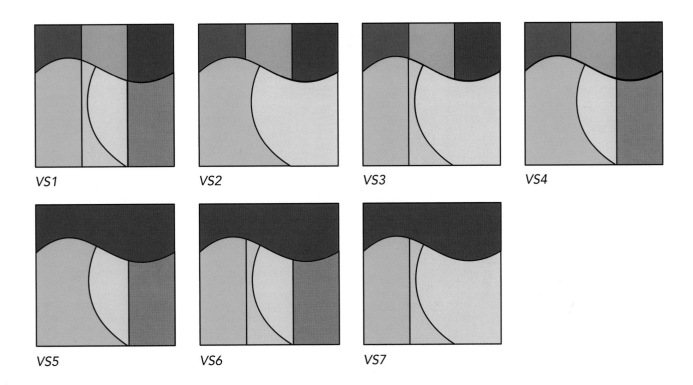

VS1   VS2   VS3   VS4

VS5   VS6   VS7

The Vertical Split Blocks: The pictures below show the blocks labeled with the template pieces that are split on the vertical lines.

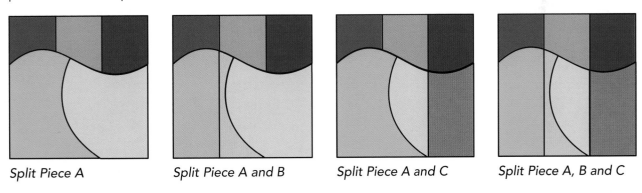

Split Piece A   Split Piece A and B   Split Piece A and C   Split Piece A, B and C

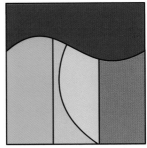

Split Piece B and C

You can see how versatile the vertical split block can be when you look at the illustration below. These two quilts are identical designs, but one fabric was changed to create two very different quilts. The pictures of the corresponding blocks used for these two quilts show that the middle fabric in the strip pieced A is blue in one block and green in the other. That one small change has a very dramatic impact on the visual appearance of these two quilts. If changing one small piece of fabric in a block can change the quilt's appearance this much, you can imagine the possibilities when you start making major changes in the fabric selections you choose.

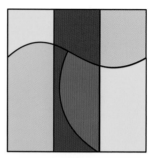 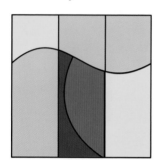

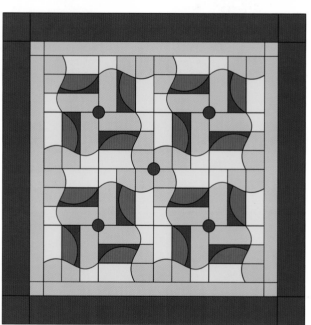

The line drawing to the right is the same design as the two quilts shown above. I have re-colored the blocks and turned the block designs in different ways to come up with all the quilt designs on page 45. This black-and-white line drawing, as well as other quilt designs, are available on the CD at the back of the book to print out on your home computer, so you can color your own split design quilts.

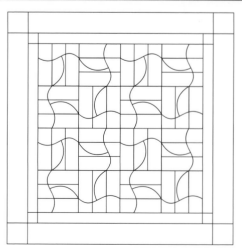

Here are examples of vertical split quilt designs with different color and design arrangements. The circles in these quilts are appliquéd circles that are applied after the blocks are sewn together.

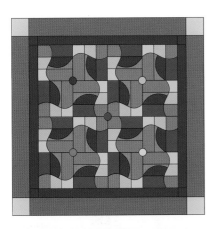
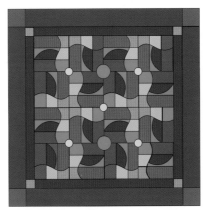
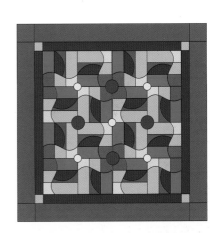
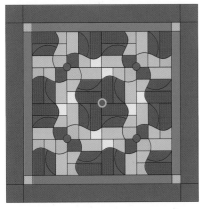
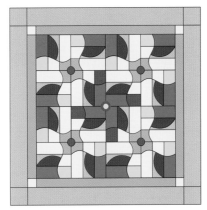
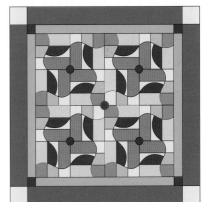
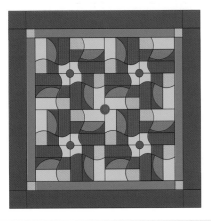
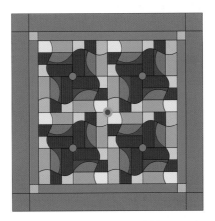
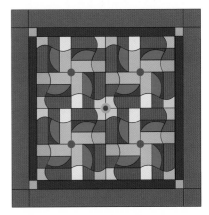

- - Single Vertical Split Piece A - -

Constructing the vertical split blocks is done the same way the diagonal split designs were done on pages 38-40. This time, you will line up the pieced-fabric strip seams on the vertical lines of your templates.

Step 1
Cut 2 strips of fabric 5" wide by the width of fabric and one strip for the middle piece 3½" wide by the width of fabric.

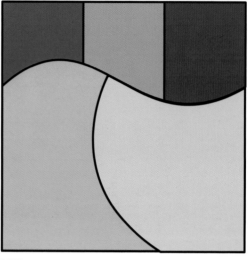

VS2

Step 2
Sew the two 5" strips on each side of the 3½" strip

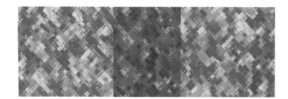

Step 3
Press open all the seams and apply spray starch to stabilize the block.

Step 4
Line up your Piece A template so that the vertical lines are aligned directly over the seam lines of the three pieces that you have just sewn together. Now cut around the template using a 28-mm rotary cutter.

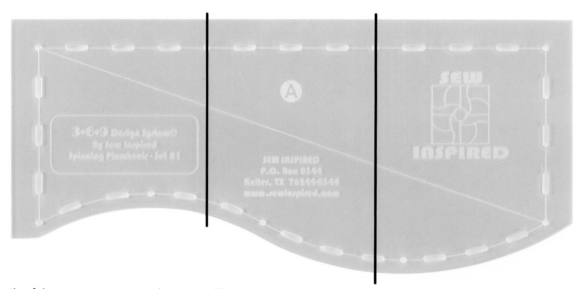

Align the fabric-strip seams to the vertical lines on the template.

- - Vertical Split Piece B - -

Step 1

Cut two strips of fabric 5" wide by the width of fabric.

Step 2

Sew these two strips together with right sides together.

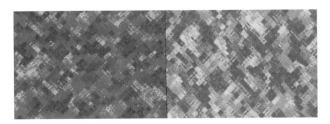

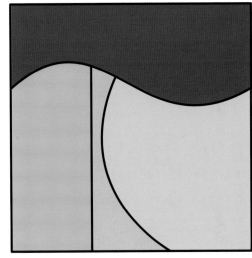

VS7

Step 3

Press open your seams and apply spray starch to stabilize the block.

Step 4

Line up Piece B template so that the vertical line on the template is directly over the seam line of the two pieces that you've just sewn together. Cut around the template with a 28-mm rotary cutter.

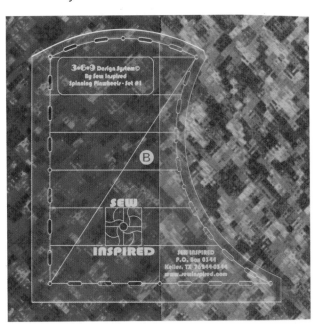

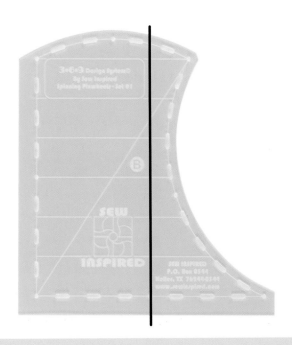

- - Single Vertical Split Piece C - -

To create the single diagonal split block C, follow the directions on page 47, but use Template C instead of Template B.

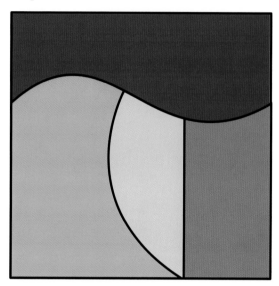

VS5

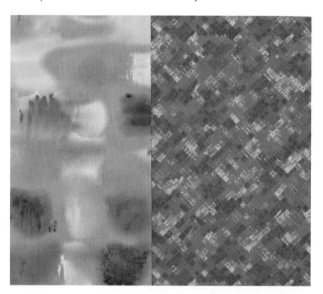

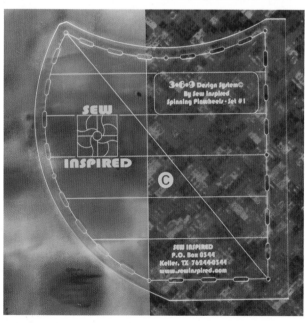

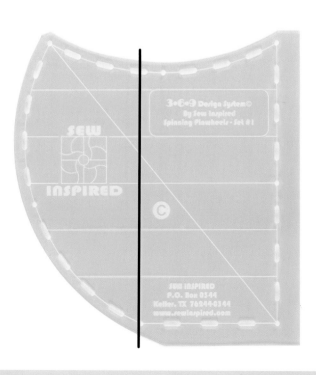

HINT

You can cut four layers of fabric at the same time. Just make sure that you have all the seam lines precisely aligned and all facing up before you cut your blocks.

- - Double Vertical Split - -

To create a block with two pieces split, follow the directions to split each piece as described above. Then piece together your pinwheel block as described on pages 27- 29. You could create a quilt splitting Piece A and C or A and B as shown below to come up with even more quilt variations.

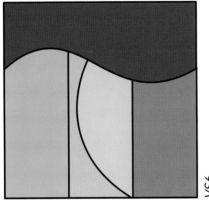
VS6

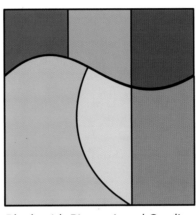
VS4

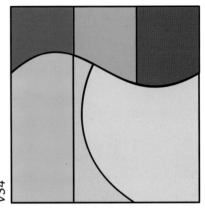
VS3

Block with Pieces B and C split   *Block with Pieces A and C split*   *Block with Pieces A and B split*

- - Triple Vertical Split - -

Here is a diagram of the triple vertical split block that has all three pieces split diagonally. Don't forget that if you are making these split designs, it is extremely important for you to heavily starch your blocks.

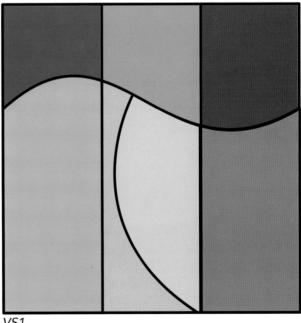
VS1

BASIC BUILDING BLOCKS

There are so many blocks that fit into the criteria of the 3-6-9 Design System that they could fill another entire book. In this chapter, you will discover 12 examples of basic building blocks that can easily be created and used in conjunction with your Spinning Pinwheel blocks. Using these 12 blocks in conjunction with all the variations of the Spinning Pinwheel blocks, the number of quilts that you can make using this system is mind-boggling.

In this section, you will find the Basic Building Block Key, which labels each block with a reference number. These reference numbers will be referred to in the project section of this book and on the CD.

Once you have learned how to make all the different variations of the Spinning Pinwheel blocks, you can start to combine these blocks with other 3-6-9 basic building blocks to create any quilt shown on the project sheets. The project sheets will show the quilt layout, each of the blocks and the quantity of blocks to make.

When you look at all the blocks on the Basic Building Block Key, there are certain components that are common across all the blocks. Each block consists of either 3" and 6" squares or 3" x 6" or 3" x 9" rectangles. If a block contains half-square triangles, the finished block will end up being a 3" or 6" square. A 3-6-9 quilt will always contain a combination of these sized components. Since the blocks will always be a finished 9", you can look at any quilt pictured in the book or CD and figure out the dimensions of the pieces and how to make those blocks. To further illustrate how the piecing works, I will demonstrate how to construct BB2 – the most complicated of all the Basic Building Blocks. Once you know how to piece this block, you can make any of the other blocks on the key. Always remember that you need to add a ¼" seam allowance to the pieces. So a 3" finished square in a quilt will be cut 3½", a 6" square will be cut 6½", a 3" x 6" rectangle will be 3½" x 6½" etc.

- - Basic Building Block Key - -

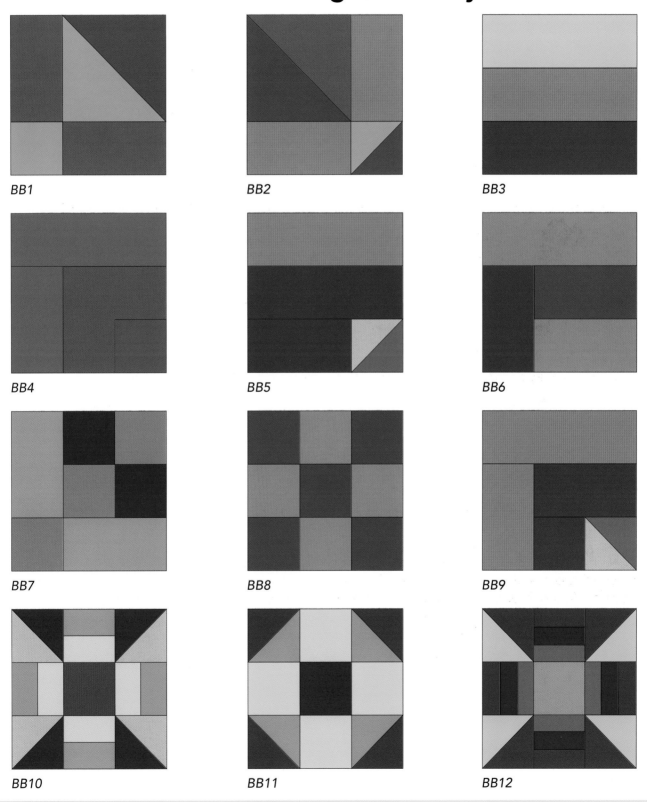

BB1

BB2

BB3

BB4

BB5

BB6

BB7

BB8

BB9

BB10

BB11

BB12

- - Piecing Basic Building Blocks (BB2) - -

CUTTING INSTRUCTIONS

Cut:

(2) 3½" x 6½" rectangle purple
(1) 7" x 7" square green
(1) 7" x 7" square* dark blue
(1) 4" x 4" square light green
(1) 4" x 4" square light blue

The cut squares are larger than 6½" and 3½" respectively, because they will be pieced and then trimmed down to a precise 6½" and 3½" square consisting of two half-square triangles. You will have one extra 6½" and 3½" square to use for another block.

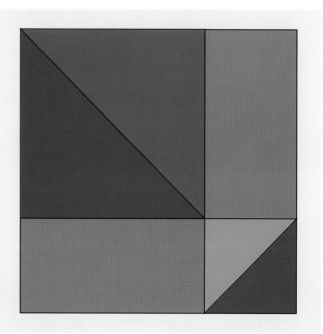

- - Piecing Two Half-Square Triangles to Make a 6½" Pieced Block - -

Step 1
Place the two 7" x 7" squares right sides together and draw a line from corner to corner with a pencil or water-soluble marker.

Step 2
Using a quarter inch foot on the sewing machine, sew ¼" from each side of the marked diagonal line, as shown in the picture below.

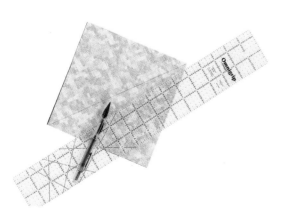

Step 3

Using a rotary cutter and ruler, cut apart the two sides on the marked pencil line. This will make two squares.

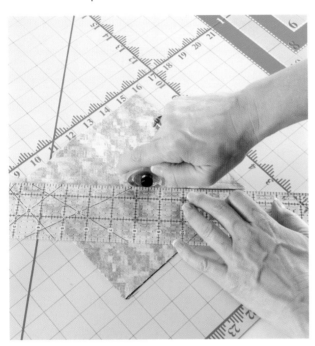

Step 4

Using a 6½" Square-it Tool or other squaring ruler, line up the diagonal line on the ruler with the diagonal seam line and cut a perfectly aligned 6½" pieced square consisting of two half-square triangles.

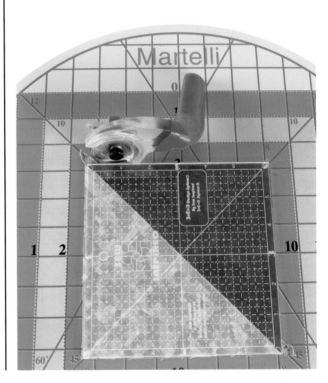

- - Piecing the 3½" Square with Half-Square Triangles - -

Step 5

Repeat Steps 1–4 above, only this time using the two 4" squares.

Step 6

Using a 3½" Square-it or other 3½" squaring ruler, follow the same direction as in Step 4 above to finish with two perfectly aligned 3½" squares consisting of two half-square triangles.

- - Piecing Building Block 2 - -

Step 7

Sew the 6½" square finished in Step 4 to one of the cut 3½" x 6½" purple rectangles as shown.

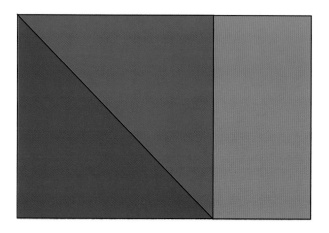

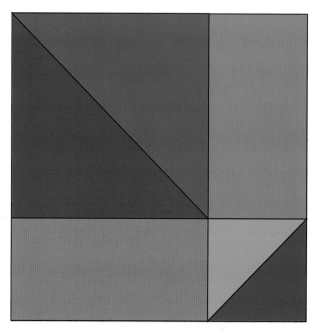

Step 8

Sew the other purple rectangle to the 3½" square finished in Step 6 so that this part of the block looks like the diagram below.

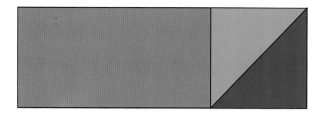

Step 9

Sew the pieces from Step 7 and Step 8 together, matching the seams to complete Building Block 2 as shown. Trim to a precise 9½" block, with all seams inside the block falling on the 3" or 6" point of the ruler.

You have just completed the most complicated Basic Building Block. Using the same method of piecing, you can construct all of the Basic Building Blocks.

You can construct all of the 3-6-9 quilts shown in this book or on the CD just by looking at the quilt and block diagrams and knowing the rules of the 3-6-9 Design System. All of the larger squares will be 6½" squares or consist of two half-square triangles that will finish at 6½". These will be made exactly the same way as the block described above. The smaller squares will always be 3½" pieced squares that will finish in the blocks at 3". Any short rectangle will be cut to 3½" x 6½", and a long rectangle will be cut at 3½" x 9½" before being pieced into your quilts. You are now ready to tackle any quilt in the Project section of this book.

DESIGN CUT QUILTS

NOTE

Design cutting (also known as fussy cutting) is cutting fabric so key elements of the fabric pattern are always visible on the finished quilt. Design cutting coordinates the fabric pattern so it works with the shapes and colors in the quilt design.

What is a Design Cut Quilt? Well, I have to admit it is not some brand new technique that I invented. In fact, design cuts have been around for a long time. It's just a technique that needs a new name. If you have been quilting a while, you have heard the term "fussy-cut." I dislike that term because the word "fussy" sounds so negative. Since I think this technique is incredibly cool, I decided it needed a new, more positive and contemporary name. When you selectively cut fabric to add design interest to your quilt, you are "design cutting," and that is the new name that I have given this wonderful technique. So from now on, when I talk about "design cutting" in my directions, you will know exactly what I am talking about.

Below are some examples of Spinning Pinwheel quilts that have used design cuts to create more interest. Piece C of the Spinning Pinwheel block was design cut to enhance the visual impact of the curved shapes.

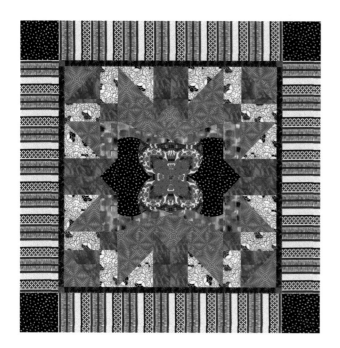

HINT

Design cut quilts are a lot of fun to make. After you have done one, you will look at your fabrics more closely to examine alternative design possibilities created by selectively cutting your fabric pieces.

- - Design Cuts Using Templates - -

Design cuts make a big difference in the appearance of your quilts. With just a little extra planning, you can turn an ordinary quilt into an extraordinary one. When I am planning my quilts, I like to look at the fabric I have selected and the shapes of my pieces to see if there are any natural fits between them. For the curved shape of template C, I like to look for fabric that will accentuate the curve in some way. In both of the quilts on the previous page, the design cuts create a look of radiating from the center. By choosing a design element in my fabric that appears to point outward, and by cutting each of the template pieces separately on exactly the same spot in the fabric each time, it appears that my Spinning Pinwheels are actually turning.

The trick to getting each design cut piece cut exactly the same way is to decide which design element you want to feature in a particular piece, and then trace the outline of that element with a marker right onto your acrylic templates. This technique will only work if you are using clear templates. After you have traced your design on the template and cut out your first piece, find the same design element somewhere else on your fabric, line up the traced marks of the element on the fabric and cut out the next piece. You cut out each piece you need for the quilt separately for this method. It's definitely more work, but the results are well worth the effort. The picture below shows the traced marks on the templates aligned to the fabric being cut.

- - Making A Design Cut Quilt - -

Fabric	Pieces to Cut	Yardage
Dark purple	(4) Piece A	¼ yd.
Dark purple (inner cornerstone)	(4) 2" x 2" squares	
Printed orange/purple	(4) Piece C	⅜ yd. *
Light purple	(4) Piece B	¼ yd.
Light orange (inner border)	(4) strips 2" x 18½"	¼ yd.*
Dark orange (outer border)	(4) strips 6½" x 21½"	¼ yd.*
Purple circles (outer cornerstone)	(4) 6½" x 6½" squares	¼ yd.*
Purple circles (circle appliqué)	(1) 8" x 8" square	¼ yd.
* These pieces are design cut and may require more yardage depending on the design repeats of the selected fabrics.		

- - Design Cut Pieces - -

The design cut quilt shown above, which we will be making in this chapter, uses design cuts in a number of places. Template Piece C, the light-orange inner border, the outer orange border, the circular appliqué, and the purple cornerstones were all design cut to add extra interest.

Step 1
Align your Piece C template over the fabric design you have selected to highlight as shown.

Step 2
Using a black permanent marker, trace the design that you have selected on to the top of your acrylic template. The marker lines can be removed with rubbing alcohol.

Step 3
Holding the template firmly in place, cut out your Piece C with a 28-mm rotary cutter.

Step 4
Cut three more Piece Cs, using the marker lines as a guide when aligning the template to the fabric.

Four identical "design cut" Piece Cs

Step 5
Cut out all the pieces listed in the cutting table. Use the quilt on page 58 for ideas on design cuts for different types of fabrics. Pay attention to the fabric designs for alignment of your templates to the selected design cut areas of your fabric.

Step 6
After you have design cut the pieces and borders described above, sew the quilt top together using the piecing directions beginning on page 68.

Step 7
Layer your quilt with batting and backing. Quilt, bind and embellish the quilt following the directions for finishing your quilt starting on page 96.

Projects

MATERIALS FOR ALL PROJECTS

Spinning Pinwheel templates
9½" Square-it Ruler
Wash Away Wonder Tape (W.H. Collins/Dritz)
28-mm rotary cutter
Cutting mat (at least 18" x 24")
Monofilament thread in clear (or smoke for dark fabrics)
Sewing machine with a ¼" foot and open-toe foot
Small scissors or snips with pointed tip
Cotton thread for piecing (neutral or coordinating color)
Quilting thread (your choice)

Fat Quarter Quilt

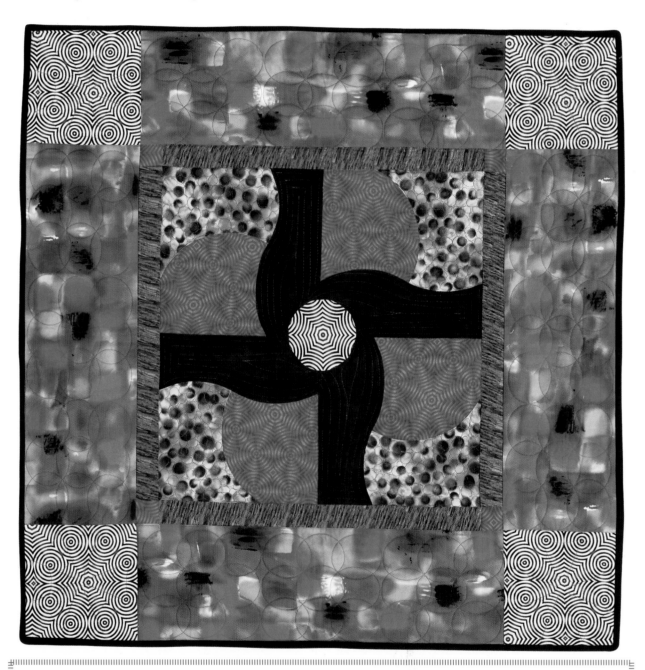

This project can be made with 6 fat quarters of fabric, 1 yard of a backing fabric and ⅜ yard for a binding fabric. The quilt makes a beautiful wall hanging that finishes approximately 30" x 30". The quilt pictured here was made using my Reflexions fabric from Blank Quilting.

MATERIALS

1 fat quarter black solid for Piece A

1 fat quarter gray dots for Piece B

1 fat quarter red circles for Piece C

1 fat quarter gray/red multi texture for inner border

1 fat quarter gray/red/black for outer border

1 fat quarter black and white circles for cornerstones and center circle

⅜ yd. black fabric for binding

1 yd. fabric of your choice backing

36" square of cotton batting

8½" square piece of lightweight stabilizer (Sulky Soft n' Sheer)

CUTTING INSTRUCTIONS

Cut:

(4) Piece A (black solid)
(4) Piece B (gray dot)
(4) Piece C (red circle)
(4) 2" x 18½" strips (gray/red for inner border)
(4) 2" x 2" squares (red circle for inner-border cornerstone)
(4) 5" x 20½" strips (red/black/gray for outer border)
(4) 5" x 5" squares (black and white circle for outer-border cornerstones)
(1) 6½" square for center appliqué
(1) 6½" square of lightweight stabilizer
(4) strips 2½" x width of fabric for binding

- - Center Squares - -

Step 1

Piece together the four basic Spinning Pinwheel blocks following the piecing instructions on page 26.

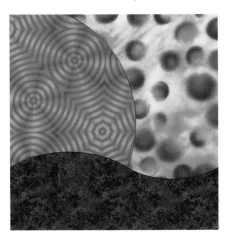

Step 2

Sew together the blocks to make row one and row two. Sew the two rows together to form the four-block center.

Row 1

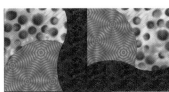

Row 2

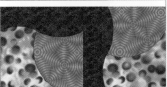

- - Inner Border - -

Step 3

Sew two of the 2" x 18½" inner-border strips to both sides of the four-block center

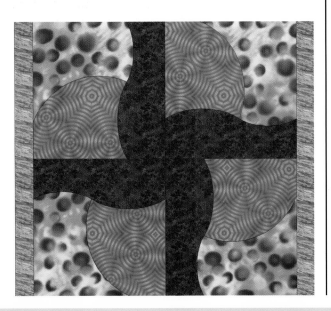

Step 4

Sew a 2" x 2" square to both sides of the two 2" x 18½" strips to complete the top and bottom inner borders, as shown.

Step 5

Sew the top and bottom inner borders from Step 5 to the section completed in Step 4.

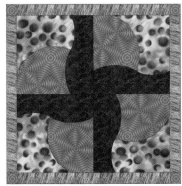

- - Outer Border - -

Step 6
Sew two of the 5" x 20½" strips to each side of your quilt top as shown.

Step 7
Sew a black and white 5" x 5" square to both sides of the remaining two 5" x 20½" strips to complete the top and bottom outer borders as shown.

Step 8
Sew the top and bottom outer border completed in Step 8 to the center section that was sewn in Step 7 to complete the piecing of your quilt top as shown.

Step 9
Apply the center circle appliqué. For instructions on applying the circular center appliqué, see embellishing instructions beginning on page 108.

Step 10
Layer your quilt with batting and backing. Quilt, bind and embellish following the instructions beginning on page 96.

Pink Dogwood Quilt

The quilt in the photograph was made with Reflexions, a line of fabric I designed for Blank Quilting. You may want to substitute fabrics and color ideas, it's up to you! The finished size of this quilt is 37½" x 37½"

MATERIALS

¼ yd. blue/green dots for Piece A

¼ yd. lime texture for Piece B

¼ yd. fuchsia circles for Piece C

⅜ yd. fuchsia texture for 1st inner border

¼ yd. turquoise for middle border

¾ yd. lime/pink/blue for outer border

⅜ yd. pink for binding

1 yd. fabric of your choice for backing

40" square of cotton batting

6½" square of lightweight stabilizer

8½" x 11" sheet of printable fabric for appliqué printable (Optional)

PC computer with color inkjet printer (Optional)

Embroidery machine, lightweight stabilizer, embroidery thread (Optional for embroidered center)

CUTTING INSTRUCTIONS

Cut:

(4) Piece A (blue/green dots)
(4) Piece B (lime green texture)
(4) Piece C (fuchsia circle fabric)
(2) 3" x 18½" strips (fuchsia texture for 1st inner border)
(2) 3" x 23½" strips (fuchsia texture for 1st inner border)
(2) 1½" x 23½" strips (turquoise for middle border)
(2) 1½" x 25½" strips (turquoise for middle border)
(2) 6½" x 25½" strips (lime/fuchsia/blue for outer border)
(2) 6½" x 37½" strips (lime/fuchsia/blue for outer border)
(4) strips 2½" x width of fabric (fuchsia for binding)
(1) 6½" square turquoise circle fabric for center appliqué (optional)

*If you don't want to print your own fabric, look for a commercial fabric with a circular motif to use for your appliquéd center, or you can use the circular machine embroidery designs on the CD at the back of the book if you have an embroidery machine. See page 116).

- - Center Squares - -

Step 1
Piece together four basic pinwheel blocks following the piecing instruction beginning on page 26.

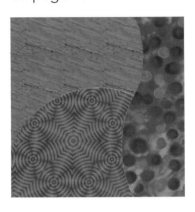

Step 2
Piece together the blocks to make row one and row two as shown.

Row 1

Row 2

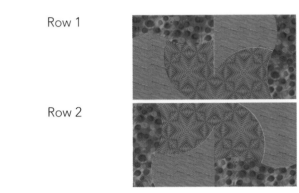

Step 3
Sew rows one and two together to form the four-block center.

- - Inner Border - -

Step 4
Sew two of the 3" x 18½" fuchsia inner-border strips to both sides of the four-block center as shown.

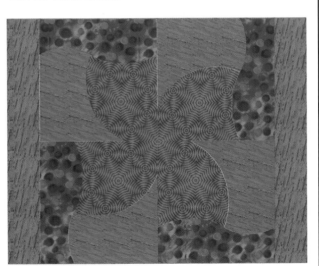

Step 5
Sew the top and bottom inner border to the section completed in Step 4.

- - Middle Border - -

Step 6
Sew the two 1½" x 23½" turquoise strips to each side of your quilt as shown.

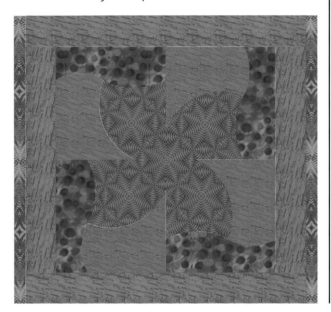

Step 7
Sew each of the 1½" x 25½" turquoise strips to the top and bottom section as shown.

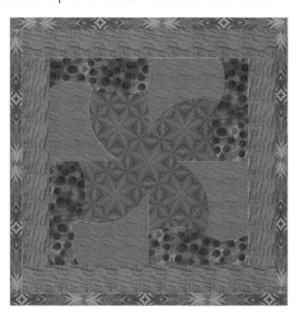

- - Outer Border - -

Step 8
Sew each of the 6½" x 25½" strips of lime, fuchsia and blue fabric to the sides of the quilt as shown.

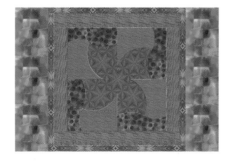

- - Center Circle Appliqué Printable - -

Step 9
Apply the center circle appliqué. For instructions on applying the circular center appliqué, see embellishing instructions on page 116. The file called AP1 works well for this quilt.

Step 10
Layer your quilt with batting and backing. Quilt, bind, and embellish following the instructions beginning on page 96.

Dogwood in a Vase

Finished size: 31" x 50"

MATERIALS

⅝ yd. orange for Piece A, B and 9½" squares

⅜ yd. turquoise for (2) 9½" squares

¼ yd. pink stars for Piece C

¼ yd. blue dots for 1st inner border

¼ yd. blue for vase

¾ yd. Lime/pink/blue for outer border

½ yd. Lime/pink/blue for binding

1½ yd. your choice for backing

¼ yd. green for stem and leaves

36" square of cotton batting

9½" square of lightweight stabilizer

8½" x 11" sheet of printable fabric for appliqué printable (Optional)

PC computer with color inkjet printer (Optional)

Embroidery machine, lightweight stabilizer, embroidery thread (Optional for embroidered center)

CUTTING INSTRUCTIONS

Cut:

(4) Piece A (orange texture)
(4) Piece B (orange texture)
(4) Piece C (fuchsia star)
(2) 1½" x 18½" strips (blue dot for 1st inner border)
(2) 1½" x 38½" strips (blue dot for 1st inner border)
(2) 9½" x 9½" squares (orange for middle lower two blocks)
(2) 9½" x 9½" squares (turquoise for bottom two blocks)
(2) 6½" x 18½" strips (lime/fuchsia/blue for outer border)
(2) 6½" x 50" strips (lime/fuchsia/blue for outer border)
(1) 5" x 12" rectangle (blue for vase appliqué)
(1) 1½" x 18" strip cut on the bias* (green for vines and leaves)
(1) 8½" square yellow fabric for embroidered center appliqué (optional)
(1) 9½" square of lightweight stabilizer

(*Cut on the bias means the strip is cut at a 45-degree angle from straight of grain)

HINT

If you don't want to print or embroider your own fabric, look for a commercial fabric with a circular motif to use for your appliquéd center.

- - Center - -

Step 1

Piece together four Spinning Pinwheel blocks following the piecing instruction beginning on page 26. Note that Piece A and Piece B are cut from the same fabric.

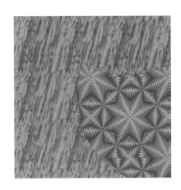

Step 2

Piece together the blocks to make row one and row two as shown.

Row 1

Row 2

Step 3

Sew rows one and two together to form the four-block center.

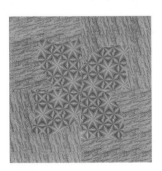

Step 4

Sew the two orange 9½" squares together to form row three of the quilt top

Step 5

Sew the remaining two 9½" turquoise squares together to make row four. Sew row four to row three.

Step 6

Sew the bottom four blocks to the top four blocks to complete the 8-block center as shown.

Row 1

Row 2

Row 3

Row 4

- - Appliqué Leaves - -

Step 7

Using the templates on the CD, trace leaf shapes onto freezer paper and cut out freezer-paper templates.

Step 8

Press freezer-paper templates onto the lightweight stabilizer and rough cut about ¾" larger than the outline of the template.

Step 9

Place freezer-paper/stabilizer layer on top of green textured fabric with right side up, and pin all layers together in the center.

Step 10

Using an open-toe presser foot, stitch right along the edge of the freezer paper completely around the leaf shape. Backstitch to secure end. Do not sew through the paper.

Step 11

Remove the freezer paper and pull the stabilizer layer away from the fabric. Carefully slit an opening in the stabilizer large enough to turn the right side of the leaf to the outside and press flat. Repeat Step 7–11 to make the second leaf.

- - Appliqué Stem - -

Step 12

Fold and finger press the cut a strip of the green bias fabric in half with the wrong sides together and sew it into a tube ¼" from the edge.

Step 13

Roll the tube so that the seam is in the back of the tube. Using your finger, open and flatten the seam so that it is positioned in the back center of the tube. Press flat with your iron.

Step 14

Position the stem in place so that it starts just below the seam point where the two pink petal seams meet. Using a seam ripper, open ¾" of the seam between the blocks, and slip the end of your stem into the seam allowance. Re-sew the seam you just opened, backstitching to secure.

Step 15

Place small pieces of Wonder Tape on the back of the stem and leaves to position and secure in place. Using monofilament thread, appliqué the stem and leaves to your quilt top using a small zigzag stitch, pinstitch or blanketstitch.

- - Appliqué Vase - -

Step 16
Fold the blue fabric rectangle in half and position the Piece A template on the fold. Cut out the vase shape with your rotary cutter.

Step 17
Place rectangle of stabilizer on top of the vase shape with right side of the fabric facing up and pin stabilizer to the fabric in the center. Sew ¼" from the edge all the way around the vase. Slit the stabilizer and turn right side of fabric out just as you did for the leaves.

Step 18
Using monofilament thread and a zigzag stitch, pinstitch, or blanketstitch, appliqué the vase in place over the bottom end of your stem. Your quilt top should now look like the picture to the right.

- - Inner Border - -

Step 19
Sew the two 1½" x 18½" inner-border strips to the top and bottom of your eight-block center.

Step 20
Sew the two 1½" x 38½" inner-border strips to the right and left sides of the eight block center as shown.

- - Outer Border - -

Step 21
Attach the 6½" x 18½" top and bottom outside border strips and then the 6½" x 50" side border strips to the quilt as shown.

- - Center Circle Appliqué - -

Step 22
Appliqué a circular motif to the center of the fuchsia flower using monofilament thread and a zigzag stitch, pinstitch or blanketstitch. See instructions on appliquéd embroidered circles or Appliqué Printables beginning on page 116.

- - Finishing the Quilt - -

Step 23
Layer your quilt with batting and backing. Quilt, bind and embellish following the instructions beginning on page 96.

Pinwheel Pillow Sham

Finished size: 22" x 22"

MATERIALS

1 fat quarter pink

1 fat quarter fuchsia

1 fat quarter lavender

1 fat quarter purple

1 fat quarter green

1 fat quarter aqua

1 yd. dark blue for border and matching back

24" square of muslin or other backing fabric

24" square of cotton batting

24" - 26" pillow form

CUTTING INSTRUCTIONS

Cut:

(2) 5" x 18" Light Pink

(2) 5" x 18" Fuchsia

(2) 6" x 18" Purple

(2) 6" x 18" Lavender

(2) 5" x 18" Light Green

(2) 5" x 18" Aqua

(2) 2½" x 18" Dark Blue

(2) 2½" x 22½" Dark Blue

(2) 22" x 14" Dark Blue

- - Diagonal Split Block - -

See instructions for diagonal split block and illustration of DS4 on page 41.

Step 1
Cut two strips of light pink and two strips of fuchsia fabric 5" x 18".

Step 2
Sew the light pink strips to the fuchsia strips.

Step 3
Press the seams open using a heavy dose of spray starch, and stack the two sets of strips on top of each other. Align the seams and pin together on the end so they don't shift while you are cutting out the template shapes.

Step 4
Line up your Piece A template so that the diagonal line on the template is directly over the seam line of the two pieced strips. Use a rotary cutter to cut both layers of fabric, making sure that the right sides of the fabric and the templates are facing up. Repeat for third and fourth piece. You should now have four of Piece A.

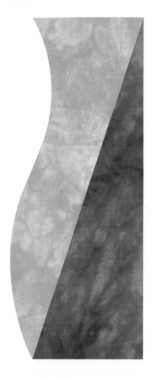

Step 5
Repeat Steps 1 - 3 using the purple and lavender fabric. Cut the strips to 6" x 18", stack the two layers and align the seams. Pin together. Place Piece B template with the diagonal line directly over the seam and cut. Repeat for third and fourth piece. You should have four of Piece B.

Step 6
Repeat Steps 1 - 3 using the green and aqua fabric. Cut the strips to 5" x 18" and stack the two layers with seams aligned before rotary cutting. Place Piece C template with the diagonal line directly over the seam and cut. Repeat for third and fourth piece. You should have four of Piece C.

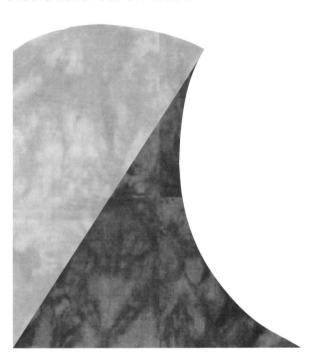

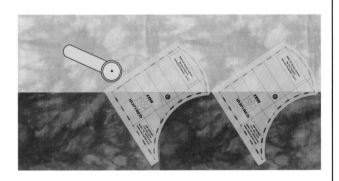

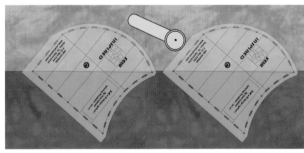

Step 7
Cut two strips of dark blue fabric 2½" x 18½" and 2 strip 2½" x 22½" for the border strips.

Step 8
Cut two pieces of dark blue fabric 22" x 14" for the Pillow back.

- - Sewing - -

Step 9

Now that you have your diagonal split pieces pieced and cut, construct four basic Spinning Pinwheel blocks using one of the methods described beginning on page 26.

Make 4

Step 10

Sew the blocks together to make rows 1 and 2. Then sew the rows together.

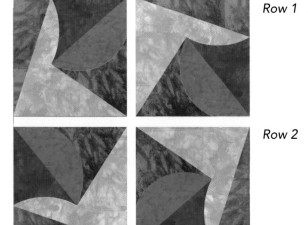

Row 1

Row 2

Step 11

Attach the top and bottom border strips. Then attach the side borders as shown.

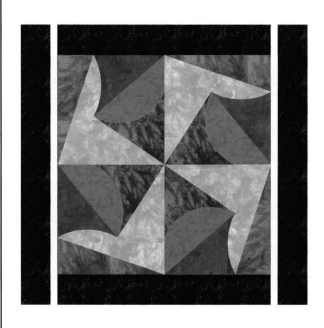

Step 12

Layer your finished pillow top with batting and backing. Quilt as desired (see page 104).

Step 13

Fold and press under ¼" along the 22" side of the two back rectangles. Then press under again ½". Stitch along the edge so that both sides will have a finished edge.

Step 14

With right sides together, lay one piece of the pillow back onto the pillow top. Match the unfinished edges to the bottom and sides of your pillow top with the finished edge across the upper center. Stitch around the three unfinished edges.

Step 15

Repeat with the other piece of the pillow back.

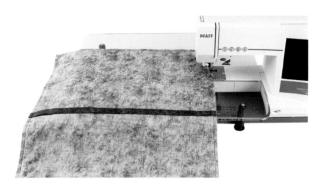

Step 16

Turn the pillow sham right side out through the opening between the two back layers and your pillow top is done!

Below are some other Spinning Pinwheel pillow ideas using different combinations of split designs. Follow the instructions for piecing the diagonal and vertical blocks beginning on page 36.

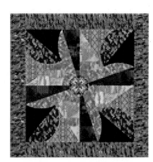

Vertical Split Quilt

You've seen just how versatile Spinning Pinwheel blocks can be when you combine split-block designs. In this chapter, we will make a wall-hanging size quilt and take the design possibilities even further by adding a coordinating block border treatment.

This quilt was made using my Reflexions II line of fabric from Blank Quilting.
Finished size: 51" x 51".

MATERIALS

½ yd. yellow for Piece A and inside block border
¼ yd. orange for Piece A
½ yd. pink for Piece B and inside block border
1 yd. navy for Piece B, inside block border, corner block and 2nd circle appliqué
⅜ yd. star focus for Piece C and center circle appliqué
1½ yd. orange/yellow for outer border
1 yd. purple for thin middle border and binding
3¼ yd. backing fabric of your choice
54" square of cotton batting
8½" x 11" sheet of printable fabric for appliqué printable (Optional)
PC computer with color inkjet printer (Optional)
Embroidery machine, lightweight stabilizer, embroidery thread (Optional for embroidered center)

CUTTING INSTRUCTIONS

Cut:

(4) 5" strips yellow fabric, (4) 5" strips orange fabric, (4) 6" strips pink fabric and (4) 6" strips navy fabric. Follow instructions on page 84 for cutting (4) diagonal split A Pieces and (4) diagonal split B Pieces.
(4) Piece C (focus fabric)

For inner border triangle blocks, cut:
(12) triangles of navy using CD template
(4) 3⅝" x 7⅞" rectangles of yellow. Then cut rectangles in half on a diagonal from one corner to the other so that you have 8 triangles or use template on CD.
(8) 3⅝" x 7⅞" rectangles of pink. Then cut in half on a diagonal from one corner to the other so that you have 16 triangles or cut 16 triangles from CD.

For inner border corner block, cut:
(2) 7⅜" squares of navy. Then cut on the diagonal from corner to corner so that you have four half-square triangles
(6) 4⅛" squares of yellow. Cut four of the squares on the diagonal from corner to corner so that you have (8) half-square triangles and (2) 4⅛" squares
(2) 4⅛" squares of navy. Cut the squares on the diagonal from corner to corner so that you have (4) half-square triangles

For outer-border corner blocks, cut:
(2) 9⅞" squares of navy. Cut the squares on the diagonal from corner to corner so that you have (4) half-square triangles
(6) 5⅜" squares of orange/yellow border fabric. Cut the squares on the diagonal from corner to corner so you have (12) half-square triangles
(2) 5⅜" squares of navy. Cut on the diagonal from corner to corner so that you have (4) half-square triangles

For outer-border strips, cut:
(4) 9½" x 33" strips of orange/yellow

For middle-thin purple border, cut:
(2) 1¼" x 33" strips of purple
(2) 1¼" x 35" strips of purple

For binding, cut:
(6) strips of purple fabric 2½" wide x width of fabric

Design cut Piece C following the instructions beginning on page 55

Cutting Directions for Pieces A & B

Step 1

Cut 1 strip of yellow fabric and 1 strip of orange fabric 5" wide by the width of the fabric.

Step 2

Sew those two strips together with right sides together using a ¼" seam allowance.

Step 3

Press the seams open using a heavy dose of spray starch. Remember, diagonal split blocks will have bias edges, so you need to stabilize them with spray starch and handle carefully during the piecing process so that the blocks don't get stretched out of shape.

Step 4

Line up your piece A template so that the diagonal line on the template is directly over the seam line. The curved edge of the template should be over the yellow side of the fabric strip. Cut around the template using a 28-mm rotary cutter. See diagonal split instructions beginning on page 38.

Make 4
Piece A

Step 5

Cut 2 strips of pink and 2 strips of navy 6" wide by the width of fabric.

Step 6

Sew those two strips together using a ¼" seam allowance.

Step 7

Press open your seams using a heavy dose of spray starch.

Step 8

Line up your piece B template so that the diagonal line on the template is directly over the seam line of the two pieces that you've just sewn together. The curved side of the template should be on the navy fabric. Cut out four Piece B pieces.

Note: Piece C is design cut out of star focus fabric.

Make 4
Piece B

- - Center - -

Step 1

Piece together four diagonal split pinwheel blocks following the piecing instructions beginning on page 36.

Step 2

Sew the blocks together to create rows one and two as shown.

Row 1

Row 2

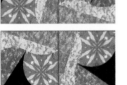

Step 3

Sew rows one and two together to form the four-block center.

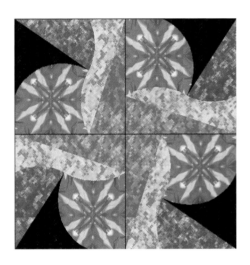

- - Inner Triangle Border - -

Step 4

Sew four of the pink and navy triangle blocks together as shown.

Make 4

Step 5

Sew eight yellow, pink and navy triangle blocks together. Four will have the pink on the left side and four will have the pink on the right side.

Make 4

Make 4

Step 6

Arrange and sew the triangle blocks completed in Steps 4 and 5 into four identical rows as shown.

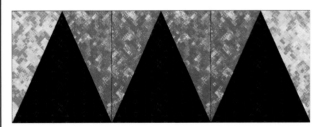

Make 4

- - Corner Flying Geese Block - -

Step 7

Place the 4¼" navy and yellow squares with right sides together, and draw a diagonal line across yellow squares. Using your ¼" foot, sew a ¼" seam on each side of the drawn line and then cut on the line. Make four squares, and press seams toward the navy fabric.

Step 8

Sew two yellow half-square triangles to both sides of the squares sewn in the Step 7 as shown.

Make 4

Step 9

Sew the navy half-square triangles cut from the 7⅜" navy squares to each of the triangles made in Step 8 so that your finished block looks like the picture below.

Make 4

Step 10

Attach the corner blocks completed in Step 7 to the top and bottom inner border row and sew the side inner border row as shown in the diagram below:

Step 11

Attach the four 1¼" purple binding strips. Sew the top and bottom strips first, then attach the side strips as shown.

Step 12

Piece the outer corner blocks following the instructions for the inner corner blocks in Steps 7 - 9 above. Attach the outer corner blocks to the upper and lower outer border strips as shown.

Step 13

Attach side outer borders and then the top and bottom borders to your quilt top as shown.

- - Center Circle Appliqué - -

Step 14

Appliqué two circular motifs to the center using monofilament thread and a zigzag stitch, pinstitch or blanketstitch. See instructions on appliquéd embroidered circles or Appliqué Printables beginning on page 118. Be sure to follow the instructions for the double appliqué technique.

Step 15

Layer your quilt with batting and backing. Quilt, bind and embellish following the directions for finishing, beginning on page 96.

Tangier Fusion

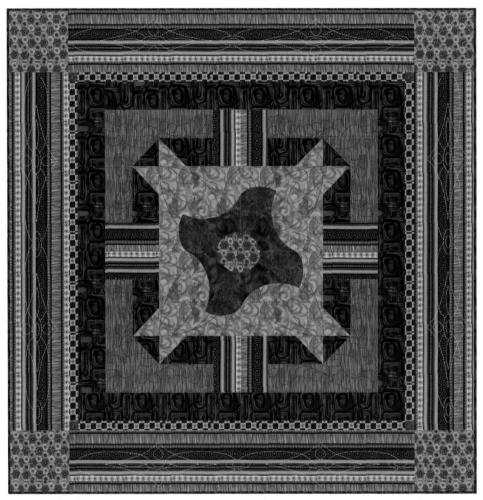

There are countless possibilities for combining the blocks in this book for exciting and beautiful quilt creations. The quilt above has a totally different look than most of the other quilts shown so far, because I combined diagonally split Spinning Pinwheel blocks with basic building blocks.

In the following pages, I will provide step-by-step directions for the quilt pictured above. At the end of the chapter, there will be a series of different quilts shown on project sheets that can be made using the same techniques. Just substitute the blocks according to the key on the project sheets. The border dimensions are equal to the dimensions of the Tangier Fusion Spinning Pinwheel quilt above.

See the Tangier Fusion layout diagram at right. The finished size of this quilt will be 51" x 51". The quilt consists of four different blocks: Spinning Pinwheel Diagonal Split DS6, Building Block 5 in two different fabric configurations; BB5 and BB5-2, and Building Block 5 reversed in the same fabric configuration as BB5-2 which are shown. See pages 120-121 for block charts.

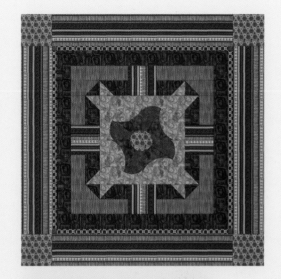

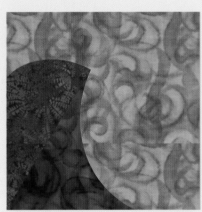

DS6 = Qty 4

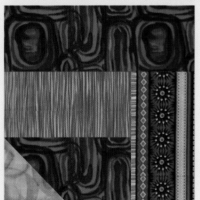

BB5-2r = Qty 4

BB5 = Qty 4

BB5-2 = Qty 4

MATERIALS

½ yd. gold swirls for Pieces A and C and half-square triangles for BB5-2, BB5-2r

¼ yd. purple texture for Piece B

¼ yd. red violet swirls for Piece B and inner-border cornerstones

1½ yd. violet for BB5 and binding

⅜ yd. orange, yellow, brown linear fabric for BB5 and BB5r

¼ yd. yellow and purple squares for inner border

1⅜ yd. striped fabric for outer border, BB5 and BB5r rectangles

¼ yd. yellow, purple, red flowers for outer cornerstone and center circle

3¼ yd. backing fabric of your choice

60" square of cotton batting

Sheer lightweight stabilizer - Sulky Soft n' Sheer is an ideal stabilizer

CUTTING INSTRUCTIONS

For center Spinning Pinwheel blocks, cut:
(4) Piece A (gold swirl)
(4) Piece C (gold swirl)
6" x width of fabric strips of both purple fabric and violet fabric. Strip piece together and cut (4) Piece B with seams lined up on diagonal line of template (see page 36)

For Building Blocks BB5, BB5-2, BB5-2r, cut:
(12) 3½" x 9½" strips (violet for BB5, BB5-2 and BB5r)
(4) 3½" x 6½" rectangles (violet for BB5)
(12) 3½" x 6½" (orange/yellow/brown for BB5, BB5-2 and BB5r)
(4) 3½" x 3½" (orange/yellow/brown)
(2) 3⅞" x 3⅞" squares (orange/yellow/brown for half-square triangles of BB5)
(6) 3⅞" x 3⅞" squares (violet for half-square triangles of BB5, BB5-2 and BB5r)
(4) 3⅞" x 3⅞" squares (gold swirl for half-square triangles of BB5-2 and BB5-2r)
(8) 3½" x 6½" rectangles (striped for BB5-2 and BB5-2r)

For inner border, cut:
(4) strips 2" x 36½" (yellow/purple for 1st inner border)
(4) 2" squares (purple for 1st inner-border cornerstones)

For outer border, cut:
(4) 39½ x 6½" strips (striped)
(4) 6½" x 6½" squares (yellow/purple/red flowers for outer cornerstones)

For center circle appliqué, cut:
(1) 8½" x 8½" square (yellow/purple/red flowers for center circle appliqué)
(1) 8½" square of lightweight stabilizer (Sulky's Soft 'n Sheer)

For binding, cut:
(6) strips 2½" by width of fabric (violet)

- - Center - -

Step 1
Piece all 16 blocks. For instructions on piecing the diagonal split block, refer to page 36. For piecing the basic building blocks, refer to page 50.

Step 2
Sew the blocks together to create rows one through four as shown.

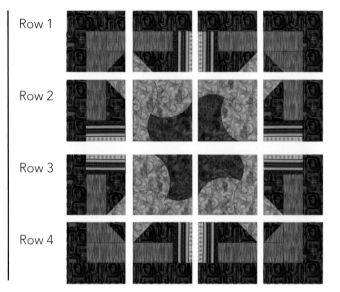

Row 1

Row 2

Row 3

Row 4

- - Borders - -

Step 3
Attach top and bottom inner borders.

Step 4
Attach the four 2" inner cornerstones to the top and bottom of the side inner-border strips.

Step 5
Attach the two inner-border strips (with the attached cornerstones) to the right and left sides of the quilt.

Step 6
Attach the two outer-border strips to the top and bottom of the quilt.

Step 7
Attach the four 6½" outer cornerstones to the top and bottom of the two side outer-border strips.

Step 8
Attach the two outer-border strips from Step 7 to the right and left side of the quilt.

- - Finishing Your Quilt - -

Step 9
To add the circle appliqué to the center of your quilt, first choose a fabric. One of the border fabrics will make a nice complement to the rest of the quilt.

Step 10
Follow the instructions on page 116 for making and applying the center circle appliqué.

Step 11
Layer your quilt with batting and backing. Quilt, bind and embellish following directions beginning on page 96.

Block Charts

On the following page I have put together a very simple Block Chart to use now that you know how to make all the variations of the Spinning Pinwheel blocks and Basic Building blocks. The enclosed CD has several more Block Charts. All these quilts will be constructed in exactly the same fashion as the Tangier Fusion. All border dimensions and finished sizes are the same as Tangier Fusion.

Each Block Chart includes a quilt diagram that shows the placement and order of all the blocks and pictures of each block,

including the quantity needed to complete the quilt. The blocks are labeled according to the block key on page 120.

The fabric chart below gives approximate yardage for quilts based on the number of blocks that you will be making. It is meant to help you estimate your fabric requirement based on your quilt design. There are sixteen additional block charts that you can print out from the CD in the back of the book. Simply select the quilt you want to make from the Quilt Gallery and then click on the print button.

APPROXIMATE YARDAGE REQUIREMENTS

# of Blocks = # of Pinwheels	Template A	Template B	Template C	1½" Inner Border Strip Sizes	Inner Border Yardage	6" Outer Border Strip Sizes	Outer Border Yardage	Finished Size w/o Borders	Finished Size With Borders
4 Blocks = 1 Pinwheel	¼	¼	¼	2" x 18½" - 4 Pieces	¼	6½" x 21½"	1	18" x 18"	33" x 33"
16 Blocks = 4 Pinwheels	⅝	¾	¾	2" x 36½" - 4 Pieces	⅜	6½" x 39½"	⅞	33" x 33"	51" x 51"
36 Blocks = 9 Pinwheels	1¼	1¾	1¼	2" x 54½" - 4 Pieces	1⅝	6½" x 57½" - 4 Pieces	1¾	54" x 54"	69" x 69"
48 Blocks = 12 Pinwheels	1⅝	1¾	1⅜	2" x 54½"- 2 Pieces & 2" x 72½" - 2 Pieces	2¼	6½" x 57½" - 2 Pieces & 6½" x 75½" - 2 Pieces	2¼	72" x 54"	69" x 87"
64 Blocks = 16 Pinwheels	2¼	2⅜	2 ¼	2" x 18½" - 4 Pieces	2¼	6½" x 75½" - 4 Pieces	2⅜	33" x 33"	87" x 87"

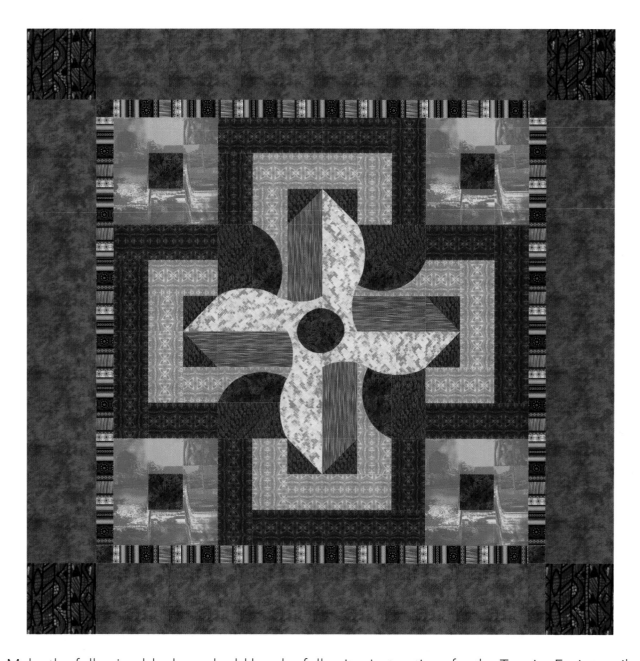

Make the following blocks and add border following instructions for the Tangier Fusion quilt beginning on page 88.

BB5 = Qty 4

BB5r = Qty 4

VS5 = Qty 4

BB7 = Qty 4

Finishing and Embellishing

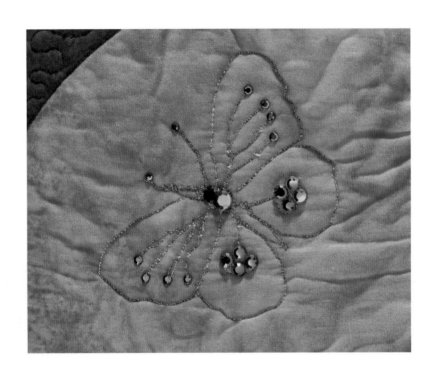

QUILTING

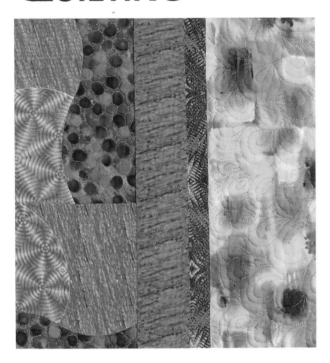

Even if you leave the quilting to the longarm quilting experts, you should still read this section so you can get new ideas and give guidance to your quilter. If you have never quilted your own quilts, I highly recommend you try it for the satisfaction and sense of accomplishment.

If you are a beginning quilter, you will need to know the basics of selecting batting and backing, layering your quilt and the various options for quilting. For experienced quilters, there are a few good tips and tricks I have learned that will be helpful and enable you to enhance your quilting skills as well.

- - Batting - -

There are many new types of batting available; it is always a good idea to ask at your local quilt shop regarding the new options available. Many of the battings that are 80% cotton and 20% polyester feel the same as the 100% cottons and work equally as well. It's important that you work with a batting that feels good to you. Batting is a personal preference. Many of the batting manufacturers have specifications and recommendation for their products on their Web sites. (See resource list at back of book.)

Cotton: Cotton batting has been my preference and is wonderful for machine quilting. I like the feel of 100% cotton. I prefer to quilt with thin cotton batting, which works well for machine quilting. Pick a cotton batting that is high quality and feels good to you.

Wool: When is it appropriate to use wool batting? If you are making a bed quilt, and you know that the person using the quilt has no allergies to wool, this would be a good choice. Wool is usually a bit more expensive, but can be well worth the price. It is wonderful to quilt with and can be a bit harder to find, but usually a good quilt shop will carry it.

Polyester: The only time I use polyester batting is when I need to add additional loft to my quilts. I use an extra layer of polyester to add loft and dimension to certain design elements in my quilts, such as in trapunto quilting, a technique that adds a 3-dimensional effect.

- - Backing - -

After you have selected your batting, you will need to figure out what you will use for your backing. The size of your quilt top will determine whether or not your backing needs to be pieced. If your quilt top is 40" wide or smaller, you shouldn't need to piece your backing. Since most fabric is around 42"–44" wide, you should be able to use a single piece of fabric as it comes off the bolt. The backing should be 3"–4" wider all around than your quilt top.

It is perfectly acceptable to piece your back. If my backing needs to be pieced, I like to use the full width of the fabric (with the selvages removed) and add an equal width on both sides of the center panel, as shown in the illustration to the right. Another option that's a bit more fun is to start out with a large center block and then cut wide strips of fabric to create a giant block, like the Log Cabin block or the Courthouse Steps block.

Side Split

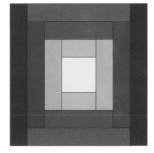

Courthouse Steps

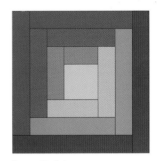

Log Cabin

If you want a quilt that is reversible, make a pieced back. I love to make the backs of my quilts look as beautiful as the fronts. People are always amazed when they turn over my quilts and find some surprises. Below is an example of a quilt where I used some of my leftovers to create a unique back.

Pieced back

- - Preparing the Quilt Sandwich - -

Now that you have selected your batting and completed your quilt back to be 3" - 4" larger than your quilt top, you are ready to layer and baste your quilt sandwich together.

Step 1
On a floor or table large enough to fit your quilt, use low-tack blue painter's masking tape to tape the backing with the right side down against the floor or table and the wrong side facing up. Starting with the top, tape from the middle out toward the sides and then repeat on the bottom. Pull taut as you tape, but be careful not to stretch the fabric. Then tape the sides down taut to the floor or table, again making sure not to stretch the fabric.

Step 2
Smooth the batting over the backing, which should be cut to the same size as the backing.

HINT
If you are using batting from a package, remove it from the package and let it hang for a day or two before you plan to use it.

Step 3
Center your well-pressed quilt top over the batting and smooth it down so that it is perfectly flat. Using the blue painter's tape, tape across the corners to secure it to the floor or table.

Step 4
Once you have your quilt sandwich taped to the floor or table, pin baste the layers together using #2 rust-proof safety pins. Pin all three layers of your quilt together about every 6" starting from the middle of the quilt and working your way out to the edges.

HINT
I like to use the specially designed curved basting pins. They are easier to close and are available at your local quilt shop.

Step 5
Once you have the entire quilt pin basted together with safety pins, you can remove the tape that is securing it to the floor or table.

You are now ready to begin quilting your quilt.

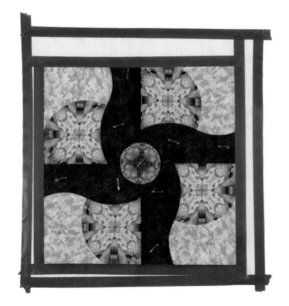

- - Stabilizing the Quilt - -

At this point, I like to take an extra step in the quilting process that makes my free-motion quilting much easier. I always stitch-in-the-ditch around any design elements that I want to emphasize in the quilt using a polyester monofilament thread in both the top and bobbin.

HINTS

Stitch-in-the-ditch means to stitch in the seam lines so that the stitching gets buried in the seam and is virtually invisible on the top. When stitching in the ditch, you should be stitching on the side of the seam that will catch the seam allowance on the underside.

When winding a clear plastic bobbin with monofilament thread, only wind the bobbin half full, because monofilament thread stretches and becomes highly compacted. If wound too full, a plastic bobbin can literally explode, releasing a messy tangle of monofilament thread.

When stitching in the ditch for stabilizing the quilt sandwich, I don't like to just stitch around the square blocks because this will emphasize the block squares rather than the quilt design. So in the case of the Spinning Pinwheel blocks, I will stitch around all the curved seams in the ditch to stabilize my quilt. Then you can remove all the safety pins before starting the free-motion quilting. This extra step frees me from having to continuously stop and remove safety pins during the free-motion quilting process. You will find that while you are doing any free-motion quilting, the more free flowing and uninterrupted the quilting process is, the better your quilting will look. If you are not planning to quilt your quilt using a free-motion technique, it isn't necessary to stitch-in-the-ditch with monofilament thread.

- - Quilting - -

There are many options for quilting your quilt. Since there are books devoted to the subject of quilting, I won't attempt to teach quilting in a few paragraphs here. But I do have a few favorite techniques that are worth mentioning.

Straight-line quilting is a great technique for a beginner. You can draw a single chalk line or press a creased line into your fabric, and then, using a quilting guide attached to your sewing machine, stitch evenly spaced lines all over your quilt.

A quilting bar makes straight-line quilting easy.

To quilt using a quilting guide, stitch first over the drawn or creased line and then set the quilting guide at the distance you want the stitching spaced. Line up the stitching guide bar so that it sits directly on top of the first stitched line and stitch the next line. Continue moving the quilting guide over each previously stitched line and continue stitching until you have covered the entire quilt vertically. Repeat in the horizontal direction if you wish.

This method can be used to stitch horizontal, vertical and diagonal rows. If you are straight-line quilting, I highly recommend that you use an even-feed or walking foot on your machine, which will hold your layers together so that your stitching will not pucker or shift layers.

HINT

Create small practice sandwiches to test tension, stitch-quality and to practice both straight-line and free-motion quilting techniques. I recommend that you practice on fabrics that have distinct lines that can easily be seen. If you can practice by following lines in the fabric, your confidence will increase and so will the quality of your quilting.

- - Free-Motion Quilting - -

In straight-line quilting, the feed dogs move the fabric through the machine. In free-motion quilting, the quilter controls the movement of the fabric. For free-motion quilting, you must lower your feed dogs and attach a free-motion foot to your sewing machine. (See your sewing machine dealer for the right foot for your machine.)

Free-motion quilting is a skill that improves with practice. I avoided free-motion quilting for a long time because I never thought I was good enough. I didn't want to ruin my quilts after spending so much time piecing them. Quilting is all about controlling the speed and movement of the fabric, and the more you practice the more control you will gain. As the mother of a 16-year-old daughter, I can tell you learning free motion is much like learning to drive a car. The first time I took my daughter out driving, we would go flying around corners way too fast, and I almost got whiplash from some of her stops. But now that she has been driving a while, she has gained control of the car and is ready for her license. Free-motion quilting is very much the same, it's all about practicing and gaining control.

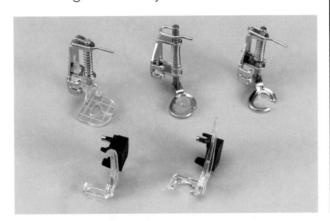

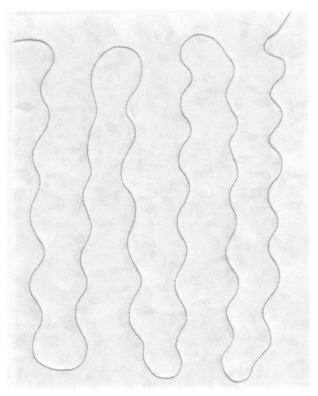

- - Imperfect Quilting for the Perfect Quilt - -

Once you are comfortable quilting accurately over the lines of the practice fabric sandwiches, you will have the control to start practicing other types of free-motion quilting designs. Here are some of the free-motion stitching designs that I use most often.

These are easy designs because they don't require any marking. I like using "rocks" in my quilting because they can vary in size, and I can keep sewing in circles until I have filled in an area. There are no perfect rocks in nature, and there doesn't need to be perfect rocks in our quilts either.

When quilting "rocks," you can sew over previously sewn circles to move through your quilt. Some quilting techniques, like "stippling," require that you never cross your lines of quilting. I don't like teaching stippling; it has too many rules. Using my imperfect design approach to quilting is much easier, more liberating and a lot more fun to do. If all the lines you sew are crooked, which is very easy to do, then all your quilting looks like you intended it to be crooked. Below are some of what I call "imperfect quilting designs" used in my Spinning Pinwheel quilts.

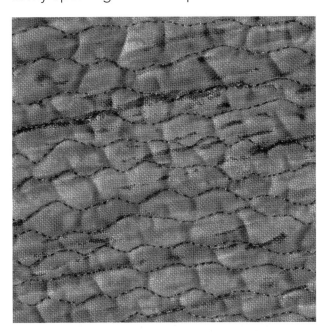

HINT

If you have an opportunity to take a workshop on free-motion quilting at your local quilt shop or through a quilt guild, I highly recommend it!

- - Blocking - -

Once you have quilted your quilt, you really should block your quilts. Blocking is done before you apply the binding to your quilt edges. To block the quilt, pin it to a design wall or lay it on a clean sheet placed over your carpet. Using T-pins, pin it perfectly flat and make sure your corners are square. After it is pinned to the floor, spray it with water from a spray bottle so that it is fairly damp, and leave it pinned flat until it is completely dry. Blocking your quilt will assure that the quilt hangs flat and won't ripple.

BINDING

NOTE

One way to enhance your binding is to put piping between the quilt and the binding. Applying piping is an extra step, but it assures that my bindings always come out perfect. I make all my own piping using a tool called the Piping Hot Binding tool. Find information on how to obtain this tool in the resources list at the back of the book.

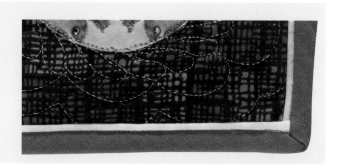

Now that your quilting is done, you are almost finished with your quilt. Applying the binding and the sleeve is the last step. For this example, we will assume a quilt that is a 45" square.

Step 1

Measure the perimeter of your quilt and add an extra 24". This allows 2" for each mitered corner and 8" tails at the beginning and end for mitering the connecting seams. Cut your binding strips 2½" wide on the cross-grain of your fabric. So, if my quilt is a 45" square, I will end up with a minimum of 208" of binding. (45" x 4 = 180" and 180" + 24" = 204".) In this case, you would cut five strips 2½" wide by the width of the fabric.

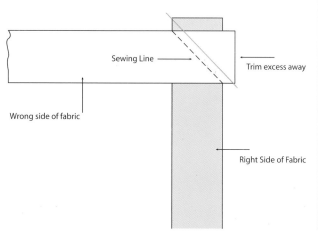

Sewing Line →

← Trim excess away

Wrong side of fabric

Right Side of Fabric

Step 2

Press the strip in half lengthwise with wrong sides together. The binding strip will now be half its original width.

Step 3

Square up your quilt sandwich by trimming away excess batting and backing. Leave ⅜" of batting and backing around the edges of your quilt. The extra batting sticking out of the edge will fill up your binding strip when you fold it over.

Step 4

If attaching a sleeve for hanging your quilt, pin the finished sleeve to the top back edge before you begin to sew on your binding. That way, the binding stitches will catch the edge of the sleeve.

HINT

A quilt sleeve is made by sewing a strip of fabric (8"–10" wide with the ends turned and stitched under) into a tube that will be about 2"–3" shorter than the width of the quilt. It is pressed flat with the seam toward the back of the tube and stitched by machine into the top edge of the quilt layered between the binding and the quilt top. The bottom of the tube is slip-stitched by hand to the quilt back.

Step 5
Align the raw edge of your folded binding strip with the raw edge of your quilt top (right sides together). Start sewing, leaving an 8" tail dangling from the quilt. You want to start at least four inches from a corner. Sew your binding strip to the quilt using a ¼" seam allowance from the edge of the quilt top (ignore the batting and backing for now).

Step 6
Stop sewing ¼" from the first corner you come to, leaving your needle down. Pivot your quilt 45 degrees and sew towards the corner. Sew right off the edge.

Step 7
Fold your strip back onto itself and then up so that the binding strip is now in line with the next edge that you are about to sew.

Step 8
Repeat the above steps around all four corners. When you reach the 8" beginning tail, stop stitching about 5"–6" from your beginning point and backstitch to secure. Remove your quilt from the machine.

Step 9
Bring the two loose tails together, line up to the edge of your quilt top, and create a miter by folding one tail up 90 degrees and the other tail down 90 degrees. The two tails should form a straight line perpendicular to the edges of your quilt.

Step 10
Press a crease at the miter point with your iron.

Fold top tail back down and pin next to where the two diagonal creases meet. Pull the unattached section of the binding away from the edge of the quilt and stitch along the creased lines to form a perfect diagonal seam to attach your binding end.

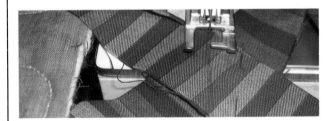

Step 11
Once you have connected your binding edges on the diagonal and are sure that your binding will fit snugly against the edge of the quilt, you can cut the extra tail away, leaving a ¼" seam allowance. Stitch down remaining unstitched binding to the quilt edge.

Step 12
Turn your binding strip to the back side of your quilt using a lot of steam. Press or pin to the back just past the stitched line.

Step 13
Machine stitch-in-the-ditch on the front side of your quilt or whip stitch by hand on the back to finish off your binding. If you have attached one edge of a sleeve into the binding edge, you will also need to slipstitch the other edge of the sleeve to the back of the quilt.

EMBELLISHING

My favorite part of the quilting process is putting on the finishing touches. Embellishing turns an ordinary quilt into a true work of art. If you plan to enter a quilt into a judged quilt show, embellishments can set your quilt apart from the rest!

An embellishment is anything you add to a quilt that gives it some extra pizzazz! It can be the thread that you use for quilting, yarn, ribbon, bead, buttons, hot-fix crystals, and other trinkets or charms that you add to the surface of your quilt.

HINT
Some types of embellishment are not suitable for bed quilts due to their usability and comfort issues.

- - Thread as an Embellishment - -

One of my favorite embellishment techniques is to use metallic threads for my quilting. Many quilters are afraid to use metallic thread because they feel that it is difficult to work with. There are a few tricks to using metallic thread that make it just as easy to use as any other thread.

- Use a Topstitch 90 or a Metafil 90 needle.
- Try skipping the thread guide that is just above the needle. On some machines, that guide shreds metallic threads.
- Using metallic thread in the bobbin when quilting with metallic thread on top will give your quilt a beautifully embellished quilt back.
- Use a test quilt sandwich with the same fabric, batting and backing of your quilt to test the quilting thread and tension. If your thread is breaking, keep loosening your upper tension until you can quilt without the threads breaking. Don't be afraid to loosen the upper tension, there are some threads that require a very loose tension. For Metallic thread, I loosen my tension dial down to 1. Check the back of the test sandwich to make sure that you have a properly formed stitch. Check with your sewing machine dealer or user's manual for specific tension settings.

- For quilting, I prefer flat metallics such as Superior's Glitter and Sulky's Holoshimmer. These threads are strong and look beautiful. The key to flat metallics is to make sure they feed through your machine without twisting. Use a horizontal thread pin adapter that feeds the thread horizontally into the machine. Vertical spool pins work on many machines as well. Just make sure that the thread feeds into the top tension disc without twisting. When I use flat metallics on top, I use a regular metallic thread that matches in color in my bobbin since winding flat metallic thread on a bobbin can be quite challenging.

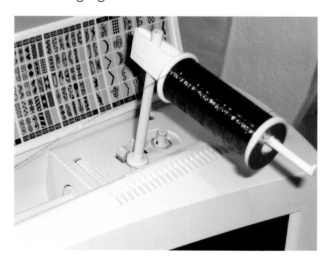

- - Bobbin Work - -

Bobbin work is a method of embellishment that can be done with free-motion embroidery, free-motion quilting, and straight, zigzag or decorative machine stitching. It is done by sewing with your quilt top face down so that the thread work on top of your quilt is actually the thread from your bobbin. Since bobbin thread doesn't have to go through the eye of the needle, you can use much heavier decorative threads, yarns or even very thin ribbon floss. A sewing machine with a separated bobbin case is better suited for bobbin work because you need to loosen the bobbin tension of your machine to accommodate the thicker threads. If you have a machine that uses a separate bobbin case, I highly recommend that you purchase a second bobbin case that you can use for adjusting bobbin tension and leave the other set for your normal sewing.

If you have a machine that has a drop-in bobbin, check with your machine dealer or owner's manual regarding adjusting the bobbin tension for bobbin work.

Bobbin work can be done at different times during the quilting process. You can embellish fabric with bobbin work even before you cut out the pieces for your quilt. You can apply it to a finished quilt top or you can quilt your whole quilt using bobbin work. Regardless of when you add bobbin work to your quilt, it will give a beautiful new dimension to the surface of your quilt. If you want to do bobbin work for your quilting and want to follow a design outline, you can first stitch the design with monofilament thread or water-soluble thread. Then, turn your quilt upside down on your machine and stitch the design over the previous stitching of monofilament or water-soluble thread.

- - Hot-Fix Crystals - -

Hot-fix crystals can add a beautiful sparkle and richness to a wall quilt. The great thing about them is that they are so easy to apply. Hot-fix crystals have pre-applied glue, so all you have to do is heat up the crystal with a special applicator to melt the glue, and place it precisely where you want it on your quilt. It only takes a few seconds to set the crystals. I recommend applying crystals after you quilt so you don't have to worry about breaking your needle on a crystal. Here are some tips for crystal placement.

- Add crystals to an embroidered design that you can add either by appliqué or directly onto your quilt top.

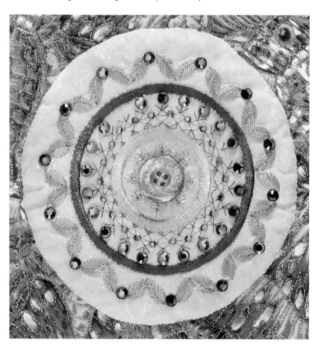

- Decorative machine stitching in the borders is perfect for evenly spaced placement of crystals.

- Use quilt designs for placement ideas.

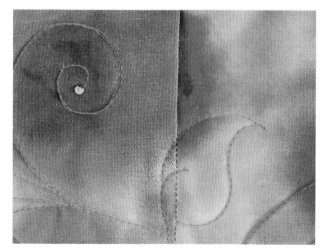

- Use designs in your fabric for placement ideas.

- Add crystals to an Appliqué Printable or other design that you can appliqué onto you quilt top.

NOTE

Plug in the applicator wand and let it heat up for a few minutes. Be sure to select a tip that fits the crystal size you are using.

Once the wand is completely heated up, pick up the crystal by placing the applicator tip on the crystal side to lift it, wait for the glue to melt (you will see the glue bubble slightly) and then tap it down quickly in the precise spot that you want to embellish.

If you are using the proper tip size, the crystal won't fall out until you tap it down onto the fabric.

HINT

Hot-fix crystals are always the last step to finishing a quilt. Add the crystals after quilting, blocking, binding and after adding the hanging sleeve.

- - Appliqués and Appliqué Printables - -

Appliqués can add spectacular interest to your quilts. Appliqués can be done as finished appliqués (see page 118) or can be raw-edge appliqués placed on your quilt with a fusible web such as Wonder Under or Steam-a-Seam. For my Spinning Pinwheel quilts, I like to use circular appliqués, because they give my quilts a central focal point.

You can also add an embroidery design as an appliqué. The picture below shows an embroidery design that has been appliquéd onto the center point of a Spinning Pinwheel design using invisible monofilament thread. The Appliqué Printables and embroidery designs are located on the enclosed CD.

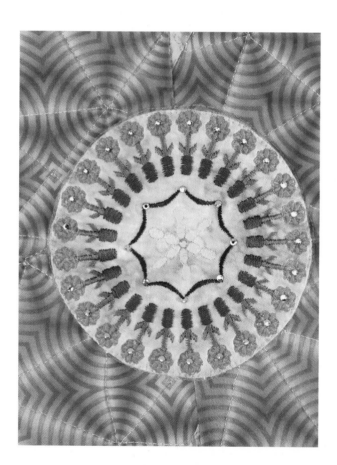

- - Decorative Stitching - -

I love to add color and extra design elements to my quilts with decorative machine stitching. Sometimes, if I can't find a fabric that has all the colors I am looking for, I will create the fabric by adding extra colors with decorative embroidery threads and decorative machine stitches. Below is a border that has been embellished with rayon embroidery thread and decorative machine stitching.

To embellish a border with decorative stitching, it is best to cut the border larger than it needs to be by a few inches. Draw a line down the center of the border with a water-soluble or chalk marking pen, and use the line as a guide for stitching a straight line of decorative stitches. Place a strip of lightweight tear-away stabilizer underneath your fabric while stitching. After the center row is stitched, use the edge of your presser foot as a guide for evenly spacing the next rows. Use matching stitches on both sides of the center stitch line for a symmetrical, balanced border.

Matching stitches on both sides of the center stitch line

- - Beads, Buttons and Charms - -

Beads and charms are another way to give texture and dimension to your quilts. Most beadwork is done by hand, but it is possible to do by machine as well. Beadwork is always done as a very last step to finishing your quilt. Beads can cover imperfections in your quilting or anything else that you may want to cover, which is true of most embellishments. I truly believe that in any art, there are no mistakes, only creative opportunities. Below are some examples of quilts that have been embellished with beads.

- - Machine Embroidery - -

Machine embroidery is another great way to embellish your quilts. I like to create circular medallion appliqués using machine embroidery which are finished into appliqués and added to the quilt top before the quilting is done. You can also use machine-embroidered quilting that is stitched through all layers of a quilt. I usually don't do machine quilting embroideries unless I am working with a smaller quilt or quilting in small sections. Below are examples of some machine quilting and machine-embroidered appliqués.

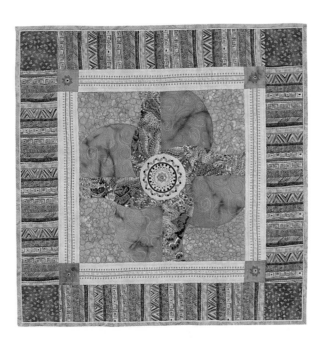

Instructions for Center Circle Appliqués

Step 1 For Appliqué Printables

Select an Appliqué Printable from the enclosed CD. Print the Appliqué Printable onto a printable fabric sheet (See sources for printable fabric on page 126. Then follow Steps 2–8.

Step 1 Using a circular motif in commercial fabric

If you are unable to or don't want to print the Appliqué Printables on the CD, select a fabric with a circular motif and follow the directions below to complete your circular center motif.

Step 1 For an embroidered appliqué

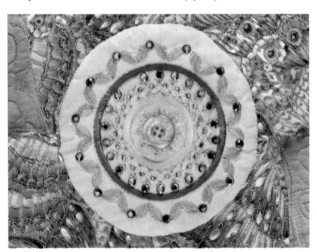

Using an embroidery machine, stitch one of the embroidery designs from the enclosed CD onto a fabric color that coordinates with your quilt.

Step 2

Place a sheer piece of stabilizer on top of the right-side-up appliqué. With a pencil, draw a circle around a CD or using a compass on the sheer stabilizer that surrounds the circular motif. If you are using an Appliqué Printable, you should be able to clearly see the edge of the circle against the white fabric background. Place a pin in the center to hold the stabilizer in place.

HINT

A sheer, lightweight stabilizer, such as Sulky's "Soft 'n Sheer," will allow you to see through it, so you can easily sew along the edge of the Appliqué Printable.

Step 3

Using a straight stitch with a small stitch length (1.5–2.0), stitch completely around the edge of the drawn circle that surrounds your circular appliqué. Do not leave any space around the circle you are stitching.

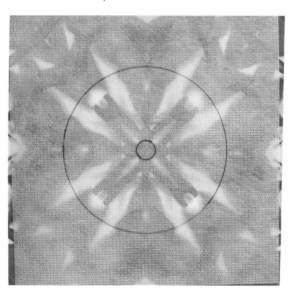

Step 4
Trim the circle completely around the stitching to about ⅛" seam allowance as shown.

Step 5
Pull apart the stabilizer and appliqué fabric in the sewn circle and carefully cut a slit about 2½" in the stabilizer.

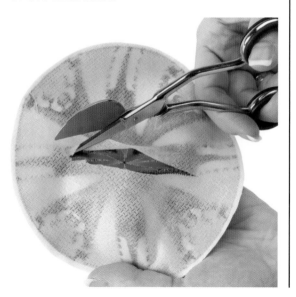

Step 6
Turn the right sides of the appliqué sewn circle to the outside through the slit and flatten and shape seams into a smooth circle.

Step 7
Press the circular appliqué flat so that none of the stabilizer is showing on the front side of the appliqué.

Step 8

Pin the finished appliqué to the desired location on your quilt top. Using a small zigzag stitch, pinstitch or blanketstitch and monofilament thread, stitch the appliqué to the quilt top by sewing completely around the circle.

HINT

If you are using light fabric, use clear monofilament thread. If your fabric is dark, use smoke monofilament thread for the best invisible stitching.

NOTE

The double-circle appliqué is created by making two appliqués in different sizes and then sewing one on top of the other.

STEP 1
Create the first appliqué as described above.

STEP 2
Create the second, background appliqué by tracing a slightly larger circle on the stabilizer.

STEP 3
Pin the smaller appliqué to the larger one and zigzag with monofilament thread. Pin both finished appliqués to the center of your quilt top and appliqué onto your quilt top.

Block Key
- - Diagonal Split Block Key - -

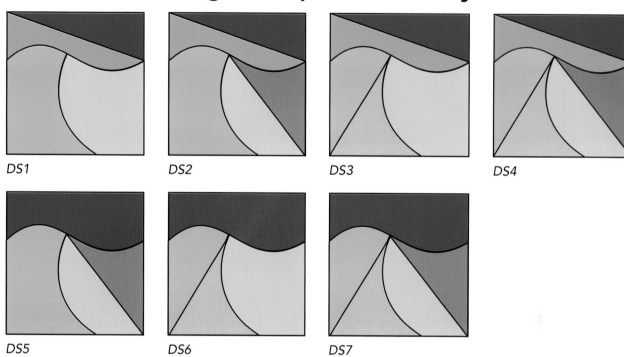

DS1

DS2

DS3

DS4

DS5

DS6

DS7

- - Vertical Split Block Key - -

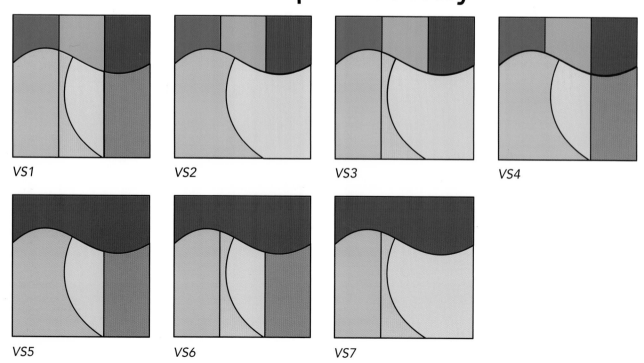

VS1

VS2

VS3

VS4

VS5

VS6

VS7

- - Basic Building Block Key - -

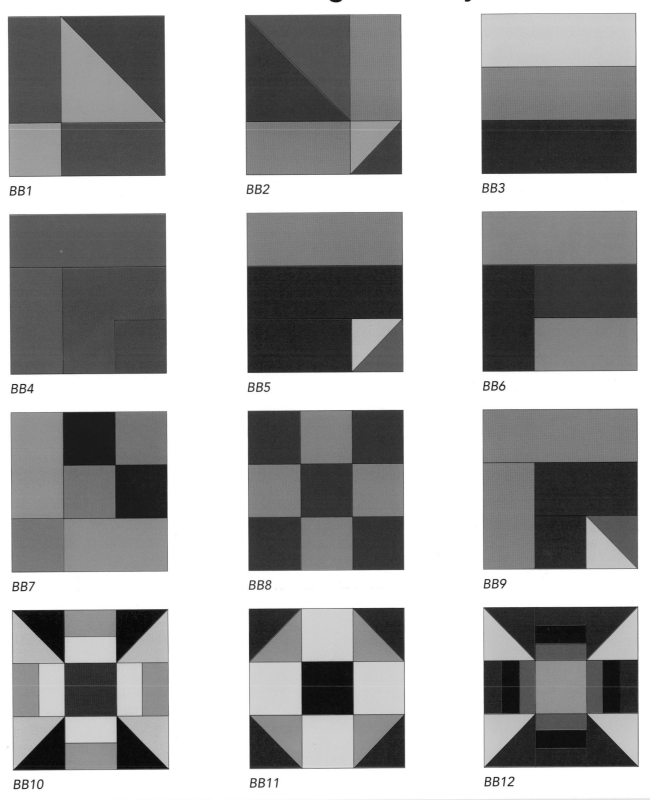

BB1

BB2

BB3

BB4

BB5

BB6

BB7

BB8

BB9

BB10

BB11

BB12

CD Contents

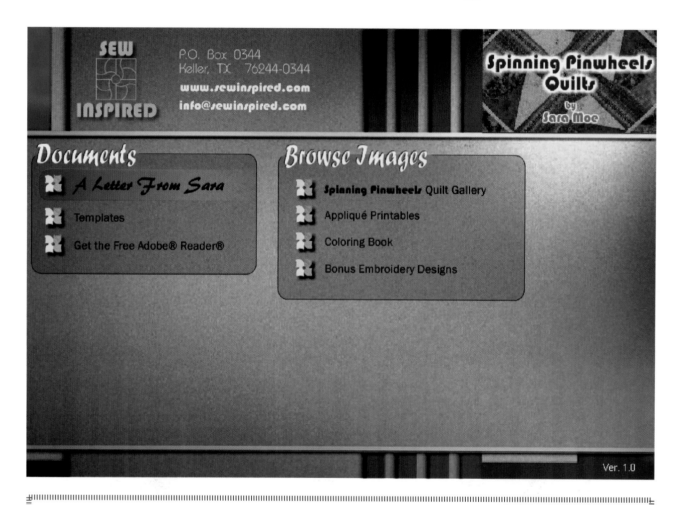

When you place the attached CD-ROM into your computer's CD-ROM drive, this is the first screen that you will see. If you don't see this screen, you can navigate to the CD-ROM by using your mouse to select Start > My Computer > SP Quilts. On the CD-ROM you will find a letter from Sara, the printable templates, and a link to download Adobe Reader—a free computer program you need to view the templates and some of the documents.

On the right side of the screen, you may select the Spinning Pinwheels Quilt Gallery, the Appliqué Printables, the Coloring Book and the Embroidery Designs.

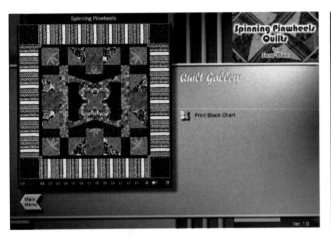

The Quilt Gallery is a gallery of ideas that contains sixteen block charts. Scroll through the photos for inspiration, and print the individual charts for specific block requirements. For instructions on using the block charts, see pages 94–95.

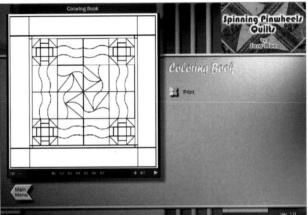

The Coloring Book features seven printable designs. Print these designs and color them with color pencils, crayons or markers before purchasing fabric to get an idea of what certain colors will look like. For help deciding on colors, see page 17.

The Appliqué Printables section of the CD-ROM features seven designs that are to be printed onto printable fabric sheets. See page 124 for pictures of the available Appliqué Printables. For instructions, see pages 112 and 116–119.

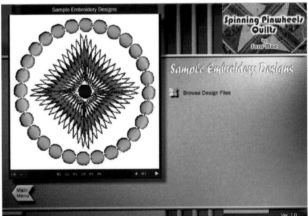

The Embroidery Designs section features six original designs in thirteen different formats. See page 124 for the available designs and pages 116–119 for instructions.

- - Appliqué Printables - -

01

02

03

04

05

06

07

- - Embroidery Designs - -

emb1

emb2

emb3

emb4

emb5

emb6

About the Author

Sara Moe's career as a fiber artist started at a very young age. In her kindergarten class, she painted a bright red flower on a pastel pink dress that her mom had just made for her, because she felt it was too pale and needed more color. Her love for bright colors and painting on fabric had early beginnings, and she continues to express herself through her brightly colored quilts, fabrics and wearable art. She started sewing her own clothes in Home Economics class in the seventh grade and has been sewing ever since.

Sara worked in the computer industry for over twenty years, and, in 2001, she finally got the opportunity to pursue her true passion when she was asked to work as a creative consultant for Pfaff Sewing Machines. That year, Sara started her own company and named it "Sew Inspired" because she wanted to spread her passion for the art of sewing and quilting by inspiring others.

Sara has traveled for the last five years teaching and inspiring sewers and quilters with her unique, out-of-the-box quilts and wearable art. She lectures and leads workshops at quilt shows and industry events for sewing machine dealers, quilt shops and guilds throughout the United States. In 2004, Sara began marketing her first quilting product when she introduced her Spinning Pinwheel Basic Design Kit, the templates used in all the quilts throughout this book. She has continued to develop her designs to create her 3-6-9 Design System.

One of Sara's newest ventures is designing her own fabrics, which combines her background in art and computers. Her fabrics are available from Blank Quilting of New York.

Sara and her quilts have been featured in numerous quilting and embroidery magazines and multiple times on the PBS Television show "America Quilts Creatively." Her work, products and descriptions of her workshops can be found on her Web site, http://www.sewinspired.com.

Resources

Sew Inspired by Sara Moe
Spinning Pinwheel Acrylic Templates and
Other 3-6-9 Design Kit Templates
Fabrics by Sara Moe
www.sewinspired.com

Blank Quilting
Fabrics used throughout this book
www.blankquilting.com

Dreamworld
Acrylic sewing machine extension tables
P.O. Box 89
County Road 21/Paradise Valley
Bonners Ferry, ID 83805
(800) 8DREAM1 or (208) 267-7136
(800) 837-3261 Orders & Info Ext. #1
FAX (208) 267-7492
E-mail: dream@dreamworld-inc.com
www.dreamworld-inc.com

Martelli Enterprise
Ergonomic rotary cutters and cutting mats
5450 North W St.
Pensacola, FL 32504
(850) 433-1414
E-mail: martelli31@aol.com
www.martellinotions.com

Old Town Quilts
Becky Harness - Longarm quilting services
140 Olive St.
Keller, TX 76248
(817) 379-4433
www.oldtownquilts.com

Pfaff Sewing Machines
31000 Viking Parkway
Westlake, OH 44145
(800) 358-0001
www.pfaffusa.com

VSM Sewing, Inc.
Husqvarna Viking Sewing Machines
31000 Viking Parkway
Westlake, OH 44145
(800) 358-0001
www.husqvarnaviking.com

Bernina of America, Inc.
Bernina sewing machines
3702 Prairie Lake Court
Aurora, IL 60504
(630) 978-2500
www.berninausa.com

Kandi Corp
Hot fix Swarovski crystals and other embellishments
P.O. Box 8345
Clearwater, FL 33758
(800) 985-2634
www.KandiCorp.com

Collins
Wonder Tape
www.dritz.com/retailers

Superior Thread
Metallic and specialty threads
87 East 2580 South
St. George, UT 84790
(800) 499-1777
www.superiorthreads.com

YLI Thread
Specialty Thread
1439 Dave Lyle Blvd. #16C
Rock Hill, SC 29730
(803) 985-3100
www.ylicorp.com

Sulky Thread
PO Box 494129
Port Charlotte, FL 33949-4129
(800) 874-4115
www.sulky.com

Press Professional
LauraStar Irons
www.laurastarirons.com

The Warm Company
Quilt Batting
(800) 234-WARM
www.warmcompany.com

Color Textiles
Printable Fabric Sheets
www.colorplusfabrics.com

Pieces Be With You
Piping Hot Binding Tool
www.PiecesBeWithYou.com

- - Additional Resources - -

Sewing/Quilting
Clotilde, LLC
P.O. Box 7500
Big Sandy, TX 75755-7500
(800) 772-2891
www.clotilde.com

Ghee's
2620 Centenary Blvd. No. 2-250
Shreveport, LA 71104
(318) 226-1701
www.ghees.com

Nancy's Notions
333 Beichl Ave
P.O. Box 683
Beaver Dam, WI 53916-0683
(800) 833-0690
www.nancysnotions.com

Quilting
Keepsake Quilting
Route 25
P.O.Box 1618
Center Harbor, NH 03226-1618
(800) 438-5464
www.keepsakequilting.com

Publications
Krause Publications
700 E. State St.
Iola, WI 54990
(800) 258-0929
www.krausebooks.com

More Skill-Building Quilt Books from Krause Publications

Quilt As Desired

Your Guide to Straight-Line and Free-Motion Quilting
by Charlene C. Frable

Take your quilting skills to new heights using straight-line and free-motion techniques. This guide features instructions for beginner to advanced quilters and a range of six projects. Discover what it means to truly quilt as desired.

Softcover • 8¼ x 10⅞ • 128 pages • 150 color photos
Item# Z0743 • $24.99

Joanie's Design Elements

8 Easy Lessons to Adapt and Use Quilting Designs
by Joanie Zeier Poole

Spend time with Joanie and your quiltmaking planning process will never be the same. Learn how to find images for a quilt, stitch in a continuous line, manipulate designs to fill empty spaces and more.

Softcover • 8¼ x 10⅞ • 128 pages • 50 color photos
Item# Z0851 • $29.99

Holiday Quilts

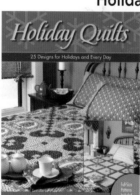

25 Designs for Holidays and Every Day
by Barbara Campbell & Yolanda Fundora

Double your quilting pleasure with this one-of-a-kind quilt book, with step-by-step instructions for creating 10+ themed quilts and home décor items for various holidays.

Softcover • 8¼ x 10⅞ • 128 pages • 225 color photos
Item# Z0746 • $24.99

Chameleon Quilts

Versatile Looks Using Traditional Patterns
by Margrit Hall, Foreword by Earlene Fowler

Learn how to use new fabrics, colors and textures and the same set of 10 quilt patterns to create 19 different projects. Features more than 200 step-by-step color photos and graphics.

Softcover • 8¼ x 10⅞ • 128 pages • 200+ color photos
Item# Z0104 • $22.99

Bundles of Fun

Quilts From Fat Quarters
by Karen Snyder

Discover fabric selection advice, instructions for making smaller quilts and adding sashing and borders in this book. Offers variations for 12 coordinating projects.

Softcover • 8¼ x 10⅞ • 128 pages • 150+ color photos and illus.
Item# FQLQ • $22.99

Call 800-258-0929 to order today!
Offer CRB7

Krause Publications, Offer CRB7
PO Box 5009, Iola, WI 54945-5009
www.krausebooks.com

Order directly from the publisher by calling **800-258-0929** M-F 8 am - 5 pm

Online at **www.krausebooks.com** or from booksellers and craft and fabric shops nationwide.

Please reference offer CRB7 with all direct-to-publisher orders.